MW01515616

Who's Sitting on Your Nest Egg?

To Aley + Gabe

Enjoy!

Robin Owen

To Alex + Gabe

Who's Sitting on Your Nest Egg?

Why You Need a Financial Advisor and Ten Easy
Tests for Finding the Best One

By Robin S. Davis, CFP

Bridgeway
Books

WHO'S SITTING ON YOUR NEST EGG?: WHY YOU NEED A FINANCIAL ADVISOR AND TEN EASY TESTS FOR FINDING THE BEST ONE
PUBLISHED BY BRIDGEWAY BOOKS
PO BOX 80107
AUSTIN, TEXAS 78758

For more information about our books, please write to us, call 512.478.2028, or visit our website at www.bridgewaybooks.net.

Library of Congress Control Number: 2007922870

ISBN-13: 978-1-933538-80-8
ISBN-10: 1-933538-80-5

10 9 8 7 6 5 4 3 2 1

This book is dedicated with love to my handsome son, Matthew, and my beautiful daughter, Brianna. Words cannot express the joy you bring to my life.

TABLE OF CONTENTS

INTRODUCTION

To make money, buy some good stock, hold it until it goes up and then sell it. If it doesn't go up, don't buy it.

WILL ROGERS

It would be nice if we could simply put that bit of investment advice by Will Rogers—the late, great American humorist—into practice. Unfortunately, without a crystal ball, it's impossible to implement, and Rogers obviously had his tongue firmly planted in his cheek when he offered it.

Ironically, at the time of his death in 1935, the United States was in the throes of the Great Depression, triggered by the stock market crash in October 1929 that wiped out the investments of millions of Americans—millions who could have avoided such a fate had they been able to follow Rogers' advice.

Today, more than seventy years after his death, learning to invest wisely has become considerably more complex than it was then. Many of

ACCORDING TO A RECENT SURVEY, NEARLY HALF OF AMERICAN CONSUMERS REPORTED THAT PLANNING FOR THEIR RETIREMENT WAS AN EVEN MORE DIFFICULT UNDERTAKING THAN RAISING THEIR CHILDREN.

today's common investment vehicles weren't available in his

day, making the road to prosperity today filled with even more detours and potholes for the unwary and unseasoned investor who embarks on the journey alone.

According to a recent survey by ING Financial Planning and Investing, nearly half of American consumers reported that planning for their retirement was an even more difficult undertaking than raising their children. Given the vast array of investment vehicles available today, the majority of them said much of the information about these products and services is simply too complex to understand.

Even with a financial advisor riding along to help navigate through the twists and turns that lie ahead, there's no guarantee of arriving safely at your destination of financial independence. Almost daily, we're reminded of that fact by the media. By now, we're all too familiar with the horror stories of the Enrons and WorldComs and other giant corporations, where the misdeeds of corporate executives left thousands upon thousands of employees and retirees without the pensions for which they had worked so hard for so long, and which they were confident would provide the independence they desired for the rest of their lives.

Sadly, even where there's been no dishonest leadership, it's become a fact of life that people can no longer rely on company pensions for financial independence. Almost daily, it seems, we read of another large corporation, which has long stood as a bulwark of successful American industry, forced by heavy losses to severely cut back or eliminate pension benefits. Almost entire industries—airlines and automobile companies, for example—have been forced to make such moves. Many of the retirees so impacted have had to find other jobs, often doing menial tasks, during what they had expected to be their "golden years."

Many other potholes and dangerous curves lie ahead. Consider Social Security, for example. As fewer and fewer workers make the payments that provide benefits to more and more retirees, the system is in grave danger, in the years ahead, of running out of funds. Everyone recognizes the problem, and there have been numerous suggestions on how to fix it, but without some major adjustments, the outgo will one day exceed the income, threatening the collapse of the entire system.

Adding to the problem is the fact that Americans are living far longer today than ever before, meaning Social Security benefits are being paid to individuals for much longer than had ever been anticipated. This added longevity poses other problems, as well. First, there's a real danger of Americans outliving their assets. Second, longer lives are often accompanied by failing health, and rising health care costs, plus the potential need for long-term care, pose serious threats to financial independence.

In their attempts to avoid these potholes, and to endeavor to improve their financial security, many investors—lured by promises of "quick" profits, "fast" cash, "ground floor" opportunities, and other enticements—head off in a new direction, only to discover they've taken a wrong turn. "Get rich quick" schemes have been around for centuries, but the only ones who do get rich are the perpetrators.

In 1912, concerns over the number of questionable promotions of stocks and other investment offers led directly to the founding of the Better Business Bureau system. Not long afterward, it adopted the slogan, "Before You Invest, Investigate," which is still sound advice for every investor.

Yet today, nearly a century later, terms like "guaranteed," "high returns," "risk-free," and "limited offer" continue to attract the unwary. In January 2006, the Council of Better Business Bureaus (CBBB) issued a media release, urging would-be investors to steer clear of risky ventures by carefully evaluating each investment proposal, its promoters, and its sales pitch.

The release included this statement by Steve Cole, CBBB president and CEO: "Every day, BBBs hear from consumers who invested in what they thought were solid and sure money-makers. They abandoned their common sense and succumbed to enticing promotions that were short on details but full of dollar signs."

Years earlier, in his typically colorful style, American newspaperman and writer Damon Runyon had sounded a similar warning to those who were tempted by these "solid and sure" schemes when he wrote: "One of these days in your travels, a guy is going to come up to you and show you a nice brand-new deck of cards on which the seal is not yet broken, and this guy is going to offer to bet you that he can make the Jack of Spades jump out of the deck and squirt cider in your ear. But, son, do not bet this man, for as sure as you are standing there, you are going to end up with an earful of cider."

Well, so much for the bad news, but that's *not* what this book is about. My purpose in writing it isn't to frighten you. There is good news! There are ways to potentially avoid these bumpy, twisting, pothole-filled roads. There are ways to avoid getting an earful of cider. There are some smooth stretches of highway that may lead you safely to your destination of financial independence, and our goal in these pages is to show you how to find and follow them.

Choosing a financial advisor is critically important—but beware! Virtually anyone can call himself or herself a financial advisor. Some are commissioned salespeople primarily intent on selling you their products, with little knowledge of, or interest in, your goals and your needs. Others are charming, articulate, and well-dressed men and women who present financial planning seminars. Many of these people may be well qualified to provide the sound investment advice and guidance you need. Others may not. How do you tell them apart?

In Part One, we outline the many reasons why you need a financial advisor, and in Part Two, we describe ten tests to help you select an advisor who has the qualifications you need, and avoid those who don't. On this journey to potential financial independence, you're sitting in the driver's seat, but having the right financial advisor sitting alongside you may give you a head start. Come along and let us show you how to pick the best one for you.

PART ONE

WHY YOU NEED A FINANCIAL ADVISOR

CHAPTER 1

NOT FOR AMATEURS

The road to the future is paved with good intentions—and littered with bad assumptions.

DAVID P. SNYDER

You've probably heard the age-old saying that anyone who attempts to serve as his or her own attorney in a legal proceeding has "a fool for a client." The message, of course, is that important legal proceedings are best left in the hands of those who've been trained in those matters.

That's good advice, which certainly applies to other professions as well. Generally speaking, unless we're trained in these specific fields, we don't try to be our own physicians, surgeons, dentists, tax accountants, or other professionals. The training required, complex and constantly changing procedures, and rules and regulations would make such endeavors foolhardy indeed.

If you're approaching retirement, or are already there, you've surely come to recognize that it's time to get serious about planning your financial future. You've read enough about financial planning to realize that it's also a complex, highly regulated, and frequently changing discipline—one that requires a great deal of time and study, and one that should not be left in the hands of the amateur.

Perhaps you're among the nearly one-half of American consumers who find that planning for retirement is a difficult task. You may be unfamiliar with financial industry jargon and have no idea what questions you should be asking or what information you need.

WHERE TO BEGIN

If that's the situation you're in, you may well be wondering where and how to begin your journey toward long-term financial independence. The road ahead can contain many potholes and pitfalls which, without competent guidance, may trap the unwary investor. Markets, both domestic and foreign, are in a constant state of flux. The number of investment products available continues to expand, with more choices available than ever before.

And, as we'll see in a later chapter, our cumbersome and confusing U.S. tax code keeps growing at such a rapid rate that even most members of Congress, the very ones responsible for writing it, can't come close to guessing just how large it has become.

Many people, not knowing what else to do, turn to that successful brother-in-law or to a friend for advice and guidance, while others recognize the need to seek professional assistance.

THE SEMINAR APPROACH

You may have received letters or flyers or brochures inviting you to a financial planning seminar or workshop; the invitation probably includes a complimentary lunch or dinner. Of course, the meal is usually served following the presentation, in the age-old tradition of "singing for your supper."

The promotional material, in whatever form, stops short of promising the moon or winning the lottery, but typically dangles such a large assortment of lures that you'd sooner skip your daughter's wedding than miss out on this once-in-a-lifetime opportunity to move on over to Easy Street.

The lures may include: a variety of ways to avoid or reduce income and estate taxes; getting *guaranteed* returns of 10 percent or more on your investments; and other "secrets" known only to the presenter.

The material invariably describes this presenter as well-known and well-educated, with many years of experience in this field. His or her name may be followed by professional sounding initials, but be careful not to be overly impressed by them. Except, perhaps, in federal government circles, you're not likely to find a more dazzling and bewildering array of acronyms anywhere other than in the financial services industry.

> EXCEPT, PERHAPS, IN FEDERAL GOVERNMENT CIRCLES, YOU'RE NOT LIKELY TO FIND A MORE DAZZLING AND BEWILDERING ARRAY OF ACRONYMS ANYWHERE OTHER THAN IN THE FINANCIAL SERVICES INDUSTRY.

In all fairness, let me emphasize that many of the kinds of seminars we've described are, in fact, presented by highly qualified and trained professionals who will serve you well. In a later chapter, we'll provide specific guidelines on how to find these well-qualified financial advisors.

SENIOR "SPECIALISTS"

Given the enormous number of baby boomers who are entering the ranks of senior citizens, it's not surprising that one of the increasingly popular designations among professionals is CSA, which stands for Certified Senior Advisor. Many of the kinds of financial planning seminars we've described above are conducted by CSAs.

In order to become a member of the Society of Certified Senior Advisors (SCSA), one must, among other things, meet certain educational requirements, subscribe to its codes of ethics and professional responsibility, participate in continuing education programs, and pass a supervised certification examination.

While those are excellent requirements, they *do not* indicate any expertise in financial planning. On the SCSA website, it states clearly that membership is open "to anyone who works with seniors," in a wide range of areas that are important to that marketplace. Among the professions it lists whose members have earned the CSA designation are clergymen, physicians, social workers, funeral directors, realtors, and insurance agents, as well as financial planners.

While the CSA whose seminar you attended, or with whom you've consulted, may be a fully qualified financial planner, that designation alone is not enough to allow you to make a well-informed decision about who will guide your financial future. And that's also true about anyone claiming to be a financial professional, regardless of the initials that follow his or her name.

ALPHABET SOUP

On its website (www.nasd.org), the National Association of Securities Dealers (NASD) lists more than sixty of these acronyms that investment advisors tack onto their names.

They range from AEP to WMS, with BCA, CFG, CFP, CSA, CWPP, FAD, FRM, MFP, PPC, QFD, RFD, and a host of others in between.

They include advisors, analysts and auditors, consultants and counselors, planners and practitioners, specialists and

> IT'S IMPORTANT TO RECOGNIZE THAT SOME OF THESE ACRONYMS ARE VIRTUALLY SELF-CONFERRED, REQUIRING NOTHING MORE THAN A HIGH SCHOOL DIPLOMA AND A BRIEF SELF-STUDY COURSE.

stockbrokers. With few exceptions, they're accredited, certified, chartered, qualified, or registered.

It all sounds rather impressive, but among the key questions you must ask are:

- By whom are they accredited, certified, or chartered?
- In what way are they qualified?
- And with whom are they registered?

It's important to recognize that some of these acronyms are virtually self-conferred, requiring nothing more than a high school diploma and a brief self-study course. Without carefully checking the qualifications of a so-called financial planner, you could unwittingly be placing your future in the hands of a person who's no better qualified than you, or your brother-in-law, are.

ON THE BRIGHTER SIDE

Let me assure you that it's not my intent to portray senior specialists, seminar providers, other financial planners—or even brothers-in-law—in a negative manner. Many may well provide you with excellent counsel and guidance on your journey toward financial independence. Nor is it my goal to frighten you with talk of the many laws and regulations which govern this field.

In fact, not all of these laws and regulations are onerous; many can be of great benefit to you. However, their sheer magnitude and complexity make it difficult for all but the professional financial planner to take full advantage of them, both in maximizing income and minimizing or eliminating taxes.

You may well be missing out on some of these favorable laws and regulations. At our firm, we're constantly on the lookout for the best investment opportunities for our clients. Unless you keep abreast of the markets on a regular basis, you need an advisor to think of every aspect and every device available. For example, I regularly tell my clients not to make any moves without checking with me first, simply because I may have a better view of the overall picture.

In a later chapter, we'll explain in detail how to choose a financial advisor who's best able to meet your specific and unique needs and goals. Who knows? That person may indeed turn out to be your own brother-in-law.

CHAPTER 2

WHAT'S IN A NAME?

If it looks like a duck, and quacks like a duck, we have at least to consider the possibility that we have a small aquatic bird...on our hands.

DOUGLAS ADAMS

It's been four hundred years or so since William Shakespeare posed the question: "What's in a name?" He went on to answer it with these world-famous words: "That which we call a rose by any other name would smell as sweet." Then, about a century ago, American poet James Whitcomb Riley conveyed a similar message, using a different analogy: "When I see a bird that walks like a duck and swims like a duck and quacks like a duck, I call that bird a duck."

Twentieth-century British author Douglas Adams, quoted above, didn't go quite as far as Riley, merely conceding that, despite all the appearances of duckiness, "it ain't necessarily so." The same thing applies to financial advisors.

If someone claims to be a financial advisor, and sounds like a financial advisor,

IN YOUR EAGERNESS TO FEATHER YOUR NEST, YOU COULD WIND UP PUTTING ALL YOUR EGGS IN THE WRONG BASKET.

you have to at least consider the possibility that you have a genuine financial advisor on your hands. But it's extremely important for your fiscal well-being to also consider the possibility that you don't, because, in your eagerness to feather your nest, you could wind up putting all your eggs in the wrong basket.

This is when the answer to the "what's in a name" question becomes extremely important. Take, for example, the name "stockbroker" or simply "broker." According to the National Association of Securities Dealers, Inc. (NASD), which has long been the primary private-sector regulator of the securities industry in the United States, there are more than 650,000 brokers, or "registered securities representatives," operating in some 5,100 brokerage firms with a combined total of more than 106,000 branch offices throughout the nation. Virtually all of these firms, under federal law, must be NASD members, subject to its jurisdiction and regulations.

WIREHOUSES

Many of these brokers work for very large firms, such as Merrill Lynch and Morgan Stanley, which are often referred to as "wirehouses." Years ago, only the largest firms, with multiple offices, could afford to link their offices by high-speed communications systems which allowed them to instantly relay key investment data to their entire staffs. In today's Age of Technology, even the smallest firms have the same capabilities, but the term "wirehouse" has survived and is still used to refer to the largest firms.

Because they comprise such a huge segment of the investment marketplace, it's extremely important to understand what these 650,000 brokers, or broker-dealers, may or may not legally do, and whose interests they primarily represent. That's not easy to do, given the fact that many of them look like ducks and quack like ducks, but choose to describe themselves as birds of a different feather, including "financial consultants," "investment advisors," and "financial advisors."

At this point, let me hasten to assure you that it's not my intention to paint brokers as villains or as shady characters to be avoided at all costs. To the contrary, the field is overwhelmingly populated by honest and reputable men and women, who represent honest and reputable firms,

> MANY BROKERS LOOK LIKE DUCKS AND QUACK LIKE DUCKS BUT CHOOSE TO DESCRIBE THEMSELVES AS BIRDS OF A DIFFERENT FEATHER, INCLUDING "FINANCIAL CONSULTANTS," "INVESTMENT ADVISORS," AND "FINANCIAL ADVISORS."

and with whom you can deal with complete confidence. However, the fact remains that, while more than a quarter of these brokers are registered investment advisers—placing them in a fiduciary role—the vast majority are not, and thus have no legal responsibility to place their clients' best interests ahead of their own.

CUTTING THROUGH THE CONFUSION

Whether or not the planner, advisor, consultant, broker/dealer, or registered representative you're dealing with has a fiduciary responsibility to you is an extremely important distinction, one that has caused a considerable amount of confusion for investors. Simply stated, a fiduciary responsibility means the investment provider has the legal obligation to place your interests ahead of his or her own.

As a result, the Coalition for Investor Education—a broad group of consumer organizations, state securities regulators, and investment services providers—published a free brochure in May 2006 to help guide investors through the process of choosing an investment services provider.

The coalition that produced the publication includes the Consumer Federation of America (CFA), North American Securities Administrators Association (NASAA), Investment Adviser Association (IAA), Financial Planning Association (FPA) and the CFA Institute.

The brochure, appropriately titled *Cutting through the Confusion*, clearly explains the differences among the various investment providers:

Securities laws recognize two types of providers—investment advisers, who are in the business of giving advice about securities, and brokers, who are in the business of buying and selling securities on behalf of customers.

Investment advisers are subject to a *fiduciary duty*. That means they have to put your interests ahead of theirs at all times by providing advice and recommending investments that they view as being the best for you...

Brokers are generally not considered to have a fiduciary duty to customers, although this standard may apply in certain limited circumstances.

Cutting through the Confusion also contains a helpful Investor Checklist, including a series of questions to ask yourself before you invest, and another series of questions to ask your investment services provider. Free copies of the

complete brochure may be downloaded from the following
website: www.consumerfed.org/pdfs/cutting_through_the_
confusion_brochure.pdf

Advisors or Sales Reps?

Part of the confusion stems from the fact that the U.S.
Securities and Exchange Commission (SEC), which is the
government agency responsible for administering federal
securities laws in the United States, has ruled that broker-
dealers are excluded from certain requirements which are
imposed on those financial professionals—such as registered
investment advisors—who do provide investment advice.
The ruling, which has been challenged in a lawsuit brought by
the 30,000-member Financial Planning Association (FPA),
is based on the SEC's assumption that whatever financial
advice brokers give to clients is "solely incidental" to their
primary job of selling securities.

The position taken by the FPA, along with several
other consumer watchdog groups, is that the SEC ruling
incorrectly relieves brokers from any fiduciary responsibilities
to their clients, giving those clients no more protection than
they receive from the folks who sell them their furniture or
automobiles.

In fact, it's probably less protection in many cases. Lots
of furniture dealers offer "no payment and no interest" for
three years from next Tuesday, and if that car you bought
turns out to be a lemon, you'll probably have at least some
warranty protection. But if that "hot" stock your broker
recommended you buy goes south, you'll be left holding the
bag—an empty one at that!

Doing Business with Brokers

In working with brokers, a primary concern is that they, being basically commissioned sales representatives, may be under real or implied pressure to recommend their own firm's products, or may face the temptation to sell securities on which they receive the highest commission, thus feathering their own nests at the expense of their clients.

Are we suggesting you avoid doing business with a broker-dealer? By no means! Rather, our goal is simply to educate you about the many different kinds of professionals who inhabit the world of investments, and allow you to make decisions that are in your best interests.

In launching a relationship with a prospective client, brokerage firms are required by the SEC to include the following statement in their new account forms: "Your account is a brokerage account and not an advisory account. Our interests may not be the same as yours. Please ask us questions to make sure you understand your rights and obligations to you, including the extent of our obligations to disclose conflicts of interest and to act in your best interest. We are paid both by you and, sometimes, by people who compensate us based on what you buy..."

> THE OVERWHELMING MAJORITY OF BROKERS ARE HONEST AND REPUTABLE. THE FACT THAT THEY EARN COMMISSIONS IS EMPHATICALLY NOT A REASON TO AVOID THEM.

The language is clear, and as we noted earlier, the overwhelming majority of brokers are honest and reputable.

The fact that they earn commissions is emphatically not a reason to avoid them. In fact, many registered investment advisors and other financial advisors and planners also receive commissions on products they sell. Some earn a combination of commissions and fees, while others are exclusively fee-based.

Sound Advice

Whether you decide to do business with a broker-dealer, a registered investment advisor, or anyone else in the financial planning field, the manner in which they earn a living should not be your primary concern. By far, the most important first step you should make is to do your homework. You have far too much at stake, both now and in the years to come, to do otherwise. We suggest you begin with the following link on the SEC website: www.sec.gov/investor/brokers.htm.

In that regard, the SEC offers this advice to investors:

Federal or state securities laws require brokers, investment advisers, and their firms to be licensed or registered, and to make important information public. But it's up to you to find that information and use it to protect your investment dollars. The good news is that this information is easy to get, and one phone call or web search may save you from sending your money to a con artist, a bad financial professional, or disreputable firm.

Before you invest or pay for any investment advice, make sure your brokers, investment advisers, and investment adviser representatives are licensed. Always check and see if they or their firms have had run-ins with regulators or other investors.

This is very important, because if you do business with an unlicensed securities broker or a firm that later goes out of business, there may be no way for you to recover your money—even if an arbitrator or court rules in your favor.

Key Questions

Before establishing a relationship with any investment firm or individual, the SEC suggests asking a series of questions, including:

- What experience do you have, especially with people in my circumstances?
- Where did you go to school?
- What is your recent employment history?
- What licenses do you hold?
- Are you registered with the SEC, a state, or NASD?
- What products and services do you offer?
- Can you only recommend a limited number of products or services to me? If so, why?
- How are you paid for your services?
- What is your usual hourly rate, flat fee, or commission?
- Have you ever been disciplined by any government regulator for unethical or improper conduct or been sued by a client who was not happy with the work you did?

Given the vast amount of information available on the Internet, doing your homework is relatively easy. We suggest you begin with the SEC website (www.sec.gov) and also check those of the NASD (www.nasd.com) and the FPA (www.fpanet.org). On those sites, and by following the numerous other links they provide, you'll find answers to all your questions, allowing you to make the wisest decisions about your financial future. Thus equipped and educated, you'll easily be able to recognize a duck when you see one.

CHAPTER 3

How Much Is Enough?

I have enough money to last me the rest of my life,
unless I buy something.

JACKIE MASON

During an interview, John D. Rockefeller—who at the time was perhaps the wealthiest man on earth—was asked: "How much money is enough?" Reportedly, Rockefeller's answer was, "Just a little bit more."

That story illustrates the position many people, especially among the boomer generation—fast approaching retirement age—are facing. They have many questions, including the one Rockefeller was asked:

- How long will I live?
- What if I outlive my resources?
- How secure is my pension?
- To what extent can I rely on Social Security in the long run?
- What if I get sick and need long-term care?
- Who can I trust to give me the proper guidance and advice?

Faced with less than comforting answers to some or all of those questions, many are likely to chase after some get-rich-quick schemes, or put their future in the hands of an advisor who lacks the integrity or experience to help them reach their goals. No matter how much or how little they have, they need just a little bit more (and then a little bit more) in order to help them sleep better at night and make the uncertain future a little less threatening.

CHASING RAINBOWS

As author, consultant, and business executive David P. Snyder wrote: "The road to the future is paved with good intentions—and littered with bad assumptions." It's also paved with dreams which have little or no chance of coming true. We read stories of people who win multi-million dollar lotteries or sweepstakes, and we watch TV commercials for casinos, showing the overjoyed lady who just won a million dollars on the quarter slot machine. Of course, they don't bother to point out that it wasn't their million dollars the lady won; every penny of it came out of the pockets and purses of the losers. In the world of gambling, it takes an awful lot of broken dreams to make another's dream come true.

"Hope springs eternal in the human breast," wrote eighteenth-century British poet Alexander Pope, and millions of Americans validate that statement every day as they line up to buy lottery tickets, or feed those slot machines. They dream their dreams and keep on hoping, never stopping to think that it's the dimes, quarters, and dollars they've lost in those machines, or the worthless lottery tickets they've bought, that have allowed a handful of others to get rich at their expense.

As someone noted, lotteries are for people who are bad at math, and so are casinos. A colleague of mine told me that when the lottery was first approved in his state, he read a news item which announced that the lottery commission had just received its first batch of printed lottery tickets. Of the 40 million tickets in that batch, 36 million had no value. That left a mere 10 percent which had any monetary value at all, most of which would be worth no more than two to five dollars. That's hardly the stuff dreams are made of. The odds of winning any significant amount are infinitesimal.

HOPE SPRINGS ETERNAL, BUT THE ROAD TO THE FUTURE IS INDEED PAVED WITH BAD ASSUMPTIONS— AND WORTHLESS LOTTERY TICKETS.

Yet, we see the pictures of the six factory workers who bought a few lottery tickets, won millions of dollars, and immediately quit their jobs. The dream does come true, we think. Hope springs eternal, but the road to the future is indeed paved with bad assumptions—and worthless lottery tickets.

PERSONAL WEALTH

In January 2006, the Consumer Federation of America (CFA) and the Financial Planning Association (FPA) released the results of two surveys on the topic of personal wealth accumulation. One survey was aimed at individual consumers and the other at financial planning professionals.

The surveys revealed that only one-half of Americans even grasp the concept of personal wealth and, surprisingly, more than 20 percent believe the most practical way to achieve wealth is to win the lottery! Among those over fifty-five years of age, that number jumps to 31 percent, a statistic that underscores what journalist and social critic H.L. Mencken once noted: "The older I get, the more I distrust the familiar doctrine that age brings wisdom." Cartoonist Tom Wilson put it this way: "Wisdom doesn't necessarily come with age. Sometimes age just shows up all by itself."

According to the CFA, a nonprofit association of 300 consumer groups with combined membership in excess of 50 million, and the FPA, the membership organization for the financial planning community, only about one-half of Americans are even aware of what personal wealth constitutes. Yet, the formula for determining it is a simple one—financial assets plus home equity and other tangible assets, minus consumer debts.

Even after learning the formula, fewer than half are even aware of approximately how much wealth they have. Obviously, it's hard to know how much money is enough if we don't even know how much—or how little—we have already!

That can be especially difficult and worrisome following the unexpected death of one's spouse, particularly if that spouse was primarily in charge of the couple's finances. For example, I was contacted by a recently widowed woman who had been referred to me for financial advice. In our initial phone conversation, she told me she was very worried because of what she estimated to be less than $100,000 of net worth.

> OBVIOUSLY, IT'S HARD TO KNOW HOW MUCH MONEY IS ENOUGH IF WE DON'T EVEN KNOW HOW MUCH— OR HOW LITTLE—WE HAVE ALREADY!

When I met with her and reviewed her portfolio, I was able to give her the good news that her personal wealth was actually about $400,000, greatly relieving the stress she was feeling. Properly invested, it would give her the financial independence she desired. Now, that may seem like an extreme case, but it's not. Instead, it underscores how unaware many people are of their personal wealth.

To find the answer, one helpful place to start is on the America Saves website. Go to www.americasaves.org and click on the "personal wealth estimator" link at the top of the home page. Then, simply fill in the blanks in order to estimate your approximate level of wealth.

According to CFA Executive Director Stephen Brobeck, "Americans should be as aware of their net wealth as their physical weight. Knowing your net wealth will help ensure that spending and savings decisions are sensible and that adequate personal wealth will be accumulated."

Dreams of winning the lottery notwithstanding, Americans are very pessimistic about their capacity to accumulate wealth. Only a fourth of those surveyed believe they could save even $200,000, while less than 10 percent believe a million dollars are within their reach.

Understandably, financial planners have a more positive view. Typically, they believe that more than 80 percent of young adults could accumulate $250,000 of wealth, and about half could reach or exceed the million dollar level. In the words of FPA Chairman James A. Barnash: "Planners know that it is easier for individuals to build personal wealth than they realize. They understand the options that are most practical for individual families to maximize their wealth-building potential."

A Double Whammy

Unlike that widowed client I mentioned above, calculating your personal wealth and finding a bonanza isn't a likely scenario—quite the opposite! Many baby boomers, along with the younger generations, find themselves struggling to make ends meet. One recent survey shows that average credit card debt is at an all-time high of more than $9,000 per household. At the same time, Americans are putting money into savings at the lowest rate in decades. According to Paul Farrell, writing in the December 2005 issue of the *Journal of Financial Planning*, "Since the early '80s America's savings rate has collapsed from 11 percent to zero as we drown in debt."

With credit card debt and savings both moving in the wrong directions, the chances for millions of Americans to achieve financial stability substantially decrease. For too many people, a comfortable and secure retirement seems like the impossible dream, as they grow "another day older and deeper in debt."

That's a bleak picture, but it can be changed, and the time to start is right now, not next week, next month, or next year. There's an old Spanish proverb that says, "By the streets of 'by-and-by,' one arrives at the house of 'never.'" Your credit card debt may seem as large as an elephant, but as we all know, the only way to eat it is one bite at a time. So grab your knife and fork and get started. And even small amounts saved regularly can grow significantly over the years.

HARD QUESTIONS

At the beginning of this chapter, we listed a series of questions many people have about financial issues which will face them in retirement. We deal with several of them—pensions, Social Security, health care, finding a planner—in separate chapters, so at this point, let's see if we can shed at least a little light on the first two: "How long will I live?" and "What if I outlive my resources?"

No one, of course, knows the answer to that first question. Life expectancy tables, compiled by the U.S. Department of Health and Human Services, do provide some clues and it's clear that we're living longer all the time. For example, male babies born in 1900 had a life expectancy of a little more than forty-six years, and females two years longer. A century later, the figures had climbed to 74.3 and 79.7 years, respectively, and keep growing by three or four months annually.

> FEDERAL STATISTICS SHOW THAT THE SPENDING HABITS OF SENIORS TEND TO DECLINE AS THEY GROW OLDER, ALLOWING THE RESOURCES THEY'VE ACCUMULATED TO LAST LONGER THAN THEY HAD ANTICIPATED.

Similar trends are shown among older adults. Men who reached age sixty-five in 2003 could expect to live, on average, nearly another seventeen years—four years longer than those who reached that age in 1950. For women, the figures are twenty and fifteen years, respectively.

Of course, like the story of the six-foot-tall man who drowned while crossing a river which had an average depth of four feet, averages don't provide any guarantees. On the one hand, poor health, injuries, and other unforeseen tragedies can end lives much earlier than expected. Conversely, growing numbers of Americans are living far longer than anticipated.

OLDER THAN EVER

Not so long ago, attaining the age of one hundred was a rare occurrence. Today, centenarians in the United States number close to 80,000, a figure that's expected to reach 130,000 by 2010, and, according to the U.S. Census Bureau's "middle" projections, will soar well past the 800,000 mark by mid-century. Others predict a figure of four million or more centenarians by 2050. About 85 percent of them today are women, and for them, today's survival rate to age one hundred is projected at an astonishing one in twenty-nine!

In his typical wise-cracking fashion, the late, great comic George Burns once offered this word of encouragement to those nearing the century mark: "If you live to the age of a hundred you have it made, because very few people die past the age of a hundred." Ironically, Burns himself lived to become a centenarian, but died a few weeks after his one hundredth birthday.

Obviously, the concern about outliving one's resources is much more realistic for those who live longer than expected. For many who've reached traditional retirement age, that's meant having to stay on the job, or going back to work after retiring from their career positions. On the brighter side, federal statistics show that the spending habits of seniors tend to decline as they grow older, allowing the resources they've accumulated to last longer than they had anticipated.

Approaching retirement, you may have dreamed of the life of luxury awaiting you in your leisure years, of around-the-world cruises, everyday golf or tennis, and being pampered at five-star resorts. While those dreams may well come true, you could find yourself beginning to slow down a bit.

FEWER NEEDS

Consider this observation by Robert Brokamp, editor of the Motley Fool's newsletter *Rule Your Retirement*. "The average 75-year-old," he writes, "doesn't require as much stimulation and entertainment. You get to a point where you don't feel like going out that much; you're happy sitting at home reading books." Clearly, that sort of activity represents far less drain on one's resources.

U.S. Department of Labor (DOL) statistics tend to support Brokamp's observation. In a 2004 survey of consumer expenditures, the DOL found that annual spending on entertainment averaged $1,863 for those in the 55–64 age bracket, dropping to $1,200 and then $600 for those in the 65–74 and 75-and-over brackets, respectively. Similar results were shown in nearly every category, including housing, transportation, food and alcohol, and clothing.

There are, of course, no easy answers to these questions, because they deal with the future, which none of us can see. But we might take some comfort from this advice offered by playwright Tennessee Williams: "The future is called 'perhaps,' which is the only possible thing to call the future. And the important thing is not to allow that to scare you."

A well-qualified financial planner can be a valuable ally in heeding that advice. There are so many complex and constantly changing factors in the world of investments that it's almost impossible for the average American to keep pace. Experienced planners can help you decrease or eliminate whatever fears you may have about your financial future.

CHAPTER 4

HEALTH CARE: FINDING THE RIGHT PRESCRIPTION

*America's health care system provides some of the
finest doctors and more access to vital medications
than any country in the world. And yet, our
system has been faltering for many years with the
increased cost of health care.*

PAUL E. GILLMOR

The good news is that we're living longer, and the potentially
bad news is that we're living longer. First the good news:
in 1900, a newborn American could expect to live 47.3 years;
in 1950, life expectancy had climbed to 68.2. By the end of
the twentieth century, overall life expectancy in the U.S. was
76.9, and women could expect to live more than five years
longer than men—according to the National Center for
Health Statistics. And each year, life expectancy statistics, as
we discussed in an earlier chapter, continue to climb.

Among the reasons we're living longer are medical advances
and greater emphasis on living healthier lifestyles—eating the
right foods and getting regular exercise. None of that is any
guarantee, of course. Even the healthiest of us can experience
illness or injury at any time, with potentially devastating
effects, not only on our health but on our bank accounts.

Now for the not-so-good news. As Ohio Congressman
Paul Gillmor points out, it's certainly no secret that the

costs of health care have been rising rapidly for years, with no slowdown in sight. If you're approaching retirement, or are already retired, the news is not only not-so-good, it's terrible—potentially catastrophic—making it imperative that you obtain health insurance that will cover you in your retirement years, especially if you plan to take, or have taken, early retirement and are not yet eligible for Medicare.

AN EXPENSIVE RIDE

Consider this: one older retired couple we know of was driving along a two-lane highway in a rural area in the middle of a sunny, summer afternoon. Suddenly, they saw a pickup truck approaching at high speed—and in their lane! To avoid an imminent head-on collision, the husband, who was driving, swerved to the right, as the pickup raced by within inches—and kept right on going.

Unfortunately, there was only a very narrow shoulder and their car flipped over, landing top-down in a ditch. The husband was quickly able to release his seat belt and get out of the car without injury, while his wife sat, upside down and suspended by her own seat belt. Rescuers were on the scene almost immediately and quickly got her out of the car.

Although her only apparent injuries were some scratches and bruises and she assured the paramedics that she was okay, they insisted on getting her to the nearest hospital. Despite her protests, she was taken by helicopter to a hospital a few miles away, where an examination confirmed that her injuries were indeed minor. The elapsed time between getting in the helicopter and being released from the hospital was less than half an hour.

The couple felt very fortunate to have escaped relatively unscathed from what could have been a deadly accident. Then, a week or so later, the bad news arrived in the form of a bill from the hospital. It included one item that really got their attention: transport via helicopter—$16,000, for a ten minute ride she didn't want and didn't need! And the person who caused the accident had disappeared.

After getting over their shock, the couple learned that their insurance would cover most of the costs of the accident, saving them from what could have been a significant personal loss.

Sadly, there's nothing unique about this story. As so many others have discovered to their dismay, even a single night's stay in the hospital, or a "routine" medical test, can cost thousands of dollars.

BROKEN PROMISES

Besides the possibility of being blindsided by an unexpected catastrophe, the skyrocketing costs of health insurance can have a major impact on retirees, or those contemplating retirement, who are not yet sixty-five, and thus don't yet qualify for Medicare. If you're in that category and are counting on having employer-paid health insurance to lighten the load, you could be in for a rude awakening.

You may have worked for the same company for thirty years or more, at least partly because of your employer-paid health insurance. After all, you'd been promised again and again that it would continue through your retirement years. But, in far too many cases, these promises of lifetime health coverage (right along with pension benefits) are being broken.

We're not talking about fly-by-night companies, but many that have long been listed as among America's most solid and trustworthy corporations. They include such names as J.C. Penney, United Airlines, General Motors, and Raytheon. One recent study found that, in 2005, nearly one in eight large American corporations had cancelled their paid health insurance benefits for future retirees, a pace that shows signs of quickening in subsequent years.

> IN FAR TOO MANY CASES, THESE PROMISES OF LIFETIME HEALTH COVERAGE (RIGHT ALONG WITH PENSION BENEFITS) ARE BEING BROKEN.

Many retirees, accustomed to paying modest if any out-of-pocket health care costs, have found themselves faced with monthly premiums of several hundred dollars, plus a higher percentage of their actual medical expenses. Instead of enjoying the comfortable retirement years they'd counted on and dreamed of for so long, they've been forced to take full-time or part-time jobs just to pay the bills. That's why it's imperative to make certain—before taking that final step into retirement—that you'll have health coverage you can count on for the rest of your life.

LONG-TERM CARE

Increased longevity also brings with it the likelihood of declining health. What provisions are being made, physically and financially, in the event we'll need long-term care? Will we be better off going into a nursing home, rather than living at home or moving in with a family member?

The possibility of developing a need for long-term care, either for yourself or your spouse, can disrupt even the most carefully designed plans for a safe and secure future. In such cases, purchasing a long-term care insurance policy can offer some measure of protection. There's a wide range of products from which to choose, and your financial planner can help guide you in selecting one best suited to your needs.

Generally speaking, purchasing this type of coverage is better done sooner than later. According to the American Association of Long-Term Care Insurance, a fifty-five-year-old individual in good health can purchase long-term care insurance for an average cost of $772 a year. For a sixty-five-year-old person, the average cost is $1,456 a year.

> IT'S IMPERATIVE TO MAKE CERTAIN—BEFORE TAKING THAT FINAL STEP INTO RETIREMENT—THAT YOU'LL HAVE HEALTH COVERAGE YOU CAN COUNT ON FOR THE REST OF YOUR LIFE.

The association's website, www.aaltci.org, contains lots of valuable information, including a planning guide, useful tips, a savings calculator, and a planning checklist. Don't allow long-term, unseen costs to derail you on your journey to a secure future.

Another very important matter to consider is determining who will have the responsibility of making critical decisions on our behalf in the event we become incapacitated. Too often, we've read of bitter feuds that have torn families apart simply for lack of proper planning.

Health care is among several extremely important issues impacting your future quality of life. It's just one of the many places where the advice of a highly qualified financial advisor may help you and your loved ones make your way safely around the potholes that await the unwary on the road that leads to the future.

A BETTER WAY?

Given the state of Medicare these days and the constantly escalating costs of health care, combined with the broken company promises to retirees, the onset of old age can be a difficult process. That lifetime of healthcare you were promised after thirty or forty years on the job may have gone up in smoke.

And here's a scary thought: There's been talk off and on for years about government subsidized health care, but we all know what happens when the government takes over a program. It's a warning many U.S. Presidents, and other leaders, have sounded over the years. More than two centuries ago, Thomas Jefferson put it this way: "A government big enough to supply all your needs is big enough to take all you have." And, more recently, Ronald Reagan gave a similar warning: "You know someone once likened government to a baby. It is an alimentary canal with an appetite at one end and no sense of responsibility at the other."

> IF YOU'RE CONCERNED ABOUT FAILING HEALTH AS YOU AGE, AND THE POSSIBILITY OF HAVING TO MOVE INTO A NURSING HOME LOOMS ON THE HORIZON, YOU COULD BE LOOKING AT COSTS OF $6,000 A MONTH, OR MORE!

The health care situation in Canada is a good example. With the government now running it, people have to wait months and even years for medical procedures they need right away. Perhaps the government feels if it waits long enough, the affliction will either heal itself or the patient will die.

If you're concerned about failing health as you age, and the possibility of having to move into a nursing home looms on the horizon, you could be looking at costs of $6,000 a month, or more! That's at least $200 a day being drained from your resources as you spend your last days or years in what, at least to some degree, is confinement!

Taking a break from such sobering issues, we'd like to share with you a story of one woman who found a creative way to deal with the question of whether or not she should move to a nursing home. We don't know the author, or whether the story is fact or fiction, but we found it amusing and hope you will too.

No Nursing Home for Me!

I'm not planning to spend my last years in a nursing home, just sitting around waiting to die. There'll be no nursing home in my future. When I start getting old and feeble, I'm going to get on a cruise ship—and stay on it.

The average cost for a nursing home can run $200 a day, or more. I've checked on prices at several of the cruise lines and found I can get a long-term discount, and a senior discount price of $135 per day. That means I'll be saving $65 a day, of which $10 or $15 will be more than enough to cover gratuities.

I'll not only be saving money, but think about all the other great benefits. I can have as many as 10 meals a day if I can waddle to the restaurant, or get room service, including breakfast in bed every day of the week, if I want it.

Most cruise ships have swimming pools, workout rooms, free washers and dryers, and shows every night. They have free toothpaste and razors, and free soap and shampoo.

They treat you like a customer, not a patient. An extra $5 worth of tips will have the entire staff scrambling to help you. If my TV quits working, or a light bulb need changing, or I want the mattress replaced—no problem! They'll fix everything and apologize for the inconvenience. There are clean sheets and towels—every day! And you don't even have to ask for them.

You don't have to worry about being bored stiff by the people sitting next to you at lunch. Every 7 to 14 days, they get off, and a whole bunch of new people come onboard.

If you fall in the nursing home and break a hip, you're on Medicare; if that happens on the cruise ship, they're likely to upgrade you to a suite for the rest of your life.

Now hold on for the best! Have you always dreamed of seeing South America, the Panama Canal, Tahiti, Australia, New Zealand, Asia, or the Hawaiian Islands? The cruise lines will have ships ready to go.

So don't look [for] me in a nursing home somewhere. My new theme song is "Anchors Aweigh!" If you want to reach me, just call shore to ship. If I'm in the pool, I'll get back to you.

Oh, one last thing before I forget. When you die, there won't be any big funeral expenses. They just dump you over the side— at no charge!

—Author Unknown

Despite some of the recent well-publicized and disturbing incidents that have taken place on a few cruise ships, that sounds like a pretty good plan to me.

CHAPTER 5

SOCIAL SECURITY:
HERE TODAY! GONE TOMORROW?

*Any man who thinks he is going to be happy and
prosperous by letting the government take care
of him should take a close look at the American
Indian.*

HUGH ALLEN

It began modestly enough, back in January 1940, when a sixty-five-year-old legal secretary named Ida May Fuller, of Ludlow, Vermont, received the first monthly retirement check issued by the Social Security Administration (SSA). The amount was $22.54. But that trickle soon became a flood, as about $16 million was paid that year to some 220,000 retirees. At the time, there were more than forty workers supporting each recipient.

The agency had been formed by Congress in 1935, during the height of The Great Depression. However, if Ida May was depressed, that $22.54 might have alleviated her condition a bit, because it was worth a lot more back then than it would be today, when it wouldn't even buy a half-tank of gas. With it, though, Ida May could have purchased 125 gallons of gas, or 281 gallons of milk, or 66 loaves of bread, or more than 750 first-class stamps. If she had been earning minimum wage, her check would have equaled nearly two weeks' pay.

Miss Fuller continued to receive her monthly benefit checks for thirty-five years, until her death in 1975. In all, she had received more than $22,000 in payments. However, that initial $22.54 check she received wasn't the first payment ever made under the new law. In its beginning days, provisions had also been made for one-time, lump-sum refund payments.

The first of these lump-sum payments went to Ernest Ackerman, a motorman from Cleveland, Ohio, who retired one day after the Social Security program took effect. A nickel had been deducted from his final paycheck for Social Security, and he later received his lump-sum benefit payment of...17 cents, a more than 300 percent return on his "investment."

Congress had formed SSA to provide retirement benefits at age sixty-five for workers in commerce and industry. The lowest numbered card, with its now familiar nine digits, was 001-01-0001, and was issued to Grace D. Owen of Concord, New Hampshire.

GOVERNMENT: DOING WHAT COMES NATURALLY

In 1937, Congress did what comes naturally in government circles—it approved the first tax to fund the program. It was a payroll tax of 2 percent, split equally between employer and employee, and limited to the first $3,000 of annual income, or a maximum tax of $30 per year for each worker. In 1939, it expanded the program to include surviving spouses and children.

It wasn't until more than a decade later that the tax rate was raised to 3 percent, followed by an increase in the ceiling to $4,200 per year. Other changes followed, which included bringing more and more people under the Social Security umbrella, providing for reduced benefits at age sixty-two, adding disability payments, and in 1966, adding Medicare, and in 1975, mandating annual cost-of-living adjustments.

Over the years, the annual income ceiling has increased steadily, and by 2006, it had reached $94,200 for Social Security taxes, with no ceiling for Medicare taxes. The percentages withheld have also increased, reaching 12.4 percent and 2.9 percent, respectively. Making matters worse, the forty to one ratio of worker to retiree has steadily worsened. It now stands at about two to one, and by 2012 it's projected that benefits paid will exceed revenues.

> THE FORTY TO ONE RATIO OF WORKER TO RETIREE HAS STEADILY WORSENED. IT NOW STANDS AT ABOUT TWO TO ONE, AND BY 2012 IT'S PROJECTED THAT BENEFITS PAID WILL EXCEED REVENUES.

Clearly, that's not a good thing. According to an old—but still true—statement: "When your outgo exceeds your income, your upkeep will be your downfall."

Is the Social Security system in trouble? Or not? In his State of the Union address on January 31, 2006, President George W. Bush stated that, "By 2030, spending for Social Security, Medicare and Medicaid alone will be almost 60 percent of the entire federal budget. And that will present future Congresses with impossible choices." Then he added this warning: "The rising cost of entitlements is a problem that is not going away. And every year we fail to act, the situation gets worse."

Adding significantly to the problem is the fact that Americans are living much longer than ever before. When the SSA was formed, the average American was expected to live until age forty-seven; today, that figure has increased by more than thirty years and continues to climb. When Ida May Fuller reached age one hundred back in 1975, having collected Social Security benefits for thirty-five years, that was quite unusual. By 2010, however, there'll be more than 130,000 American centenarians, collecting far more in benefits that the system was ever designed to handle.

The debate rages on, and it has become clear to virtually everyone that drastic changes, in some form or another, will be needed in order to keep the system solvent. According to a number of surveys, a large percentage of baby boomers, along with younger generations—known by such often overlapping and confusing terms as Gen Xers, Tweeners, Mosaics, Echo Boomers, Gen Yers, Millennials and/or Baby Busters—understandably express serious doubts about the viability of Social Security over the long term.

> A LARGE PERCENTAGE OF BABY BOOMERS, ALONG WITH YOUNGER GENERATIONS, UNDERSTANDABLY EXPRESS SERIOUS DOUBTS ABOUT THE VIABILITY OF SOCIAL SECURITY OVER THE LONG TERM.

WHEN TO BEGIN

In determining when to begin receiving Social Security retirement benefits, there are a number of important options for you to consider. The first is when you want to begin receiving benefits, with the earliest possible time being at age sixty-two. Conversely, the latest possible time to begin receiving them is at age seventy.

Within that eight-year period, there are a number of factors which come into play, depending on whether or not you plan to continue working during that time. While many people elect to begin receiving benefits at sixty-two, the amounts they receive will be less than if they had waited until their full retirement age. And, if they continue to work, they'll be limited in the amount they can earn without incurring some loss of benefits.

In 2006, for example, the limit was $12,480, and it increases by about three hundred dollars each year. If you're less than full retirement age, are receiving Social Security retirement benefits, and earn more than that amount, $1 in benefits will be reduced for each $2 you earn in excess of $12,480.

FULL RETIREMENT AGE

For many years, the Social Security Administration (SSA) had defined full retirement age as sixty-five. Then, in 1983, Congress passed legislation establishing a gradual increase in the full retirement age beginning in 2000, depending on the year of birth. For those born in 1937 or earlier, it remained at age sixty-five. From 1938 through 1942, it increased by two months per year. For those born between 1943 and 1954, the full retirement age is sixty-six. Beginning in 1955, it again began an annual two-month increase. For those born in 1960 and later, the full retirement age is fixed at age sixty-seven. Once you reach full retirement age, there's no limit on how much additional income you can earn.

Delaying benefits can have a distinct advantage, especially if you continue to work. If you decide to start them at age sixty-two, your benefits would be reduced by 20 to 25 percent, or more, than if you'd waited until reaching your full retirement age. And they'll remain at that level permanently, regardless of how long you live.

If you wait until your full retirement age, your benefit payments will not only be greater, but the earnings limitations incurred at any earlier age, and the penalties for exceeding those limits, no longer apply. From that point on, you're free to earn as much as possible and still receive your full benefits.

Another factor to consider is whether to delay receiving benefits until some time after you reach full retirement age. For example, if you were born in 1943 or later, your benefits will increase by 8 percent per year until you decide to take them or reach age seventy, at which time they must begin.

What's the best time for you to begin? There are numerous other factors that come into play. Yes, the benefits at age sixty-two will be significantly less. But, if you take the money then, you'll be receiving payments over a greater number of years, and may be able to invest those funds at a higher rate of return than if you'd waited to begin. Conversely, if you're making significantly more than

> YOUR HEALTH, YOUR LIFE EXPECTANCY, AND WHETHER OR NOT YOU'RE MARRIED, ARE JUST SOME OF THE ISSUES WHICH MUST BE FACTORED INTO YOUR DECISION ABOUT WHEN TO BEGIN TAKING YOUR SOCIAL SECURITY BENEFITS.

the SSA limits, applying for early benefits makes no sense, because you'll be giving some or all of it back.

Your health, your life expectancy, and whether or not you're married, are just some of the issues which must be factored into your decision about when to begin taking your Social Security benefits. For example, both spousal and survivor benefits will be impacted based on when you start receiving payments. It can get complicated, but a well-qualified financial planner can guide you through the maze and help you find the right road to take for yourself and for your family.

MORE BAD NEWS

The existing Social Security system is clearly on shaky ground, leading many boomers and younger generations to conclude that future benefits amount to little more than "pie in the sky." Admittedly, its survival in its current state is unsustainable over the long haul, but it seems almost inconceivable that the federal government would abandon it altogether.

Some major changes must be made, not all of which are likely to favor future generations. And there's possibly more bad news regarding Social Security that would impact boomers, which may come as quite a shock to them. While Social Security benefits have generally been protected from seizure, the Supreme Court, in December 2005, unanimously ruled that a law passed by Congress in 1996 is valid.

That law allows the government to seize a portion of Social Security benefits to repay defaulted student loans. There's more than $7 billion of them on the government's books, and as the late U.S. Senator Everett McKinley Dirksen once wryly noted: "A billion here and a billion there, and pretty soon you're talking about real money."

For some time now, the government has been quietly recouping some of that real money—about $400 million a year so far—by withholding a portion of Social Security benefits. Boomers with defaulted student loans in their past could lose up to 15 percent of their monthly benefits, payments many of them have been counting on as a significant part of their retirement income.

No matter what remedies may be applied in future days to try and keep the Social Security system viable, there are serious leaks in that bucket. Prudent retirees, and those approaching that stage in their lives, would be wise to build their nest eggs from more solid materials.

CHAPTER 6

PENSIONS:
THE STUFF OF DREAMS OR NIGHTMARES?

Hold fast to dreams,
For if dreams die
Life is a broken-winged bird
That cannot fly.

LANGSTON HUGHES

Once upon a time, there was the Great American Dream. Beginning in the mid-nineteenth and continuing through most of the twentieth century, millions of immigrants flocked to the United States—the land of opportunity—with visions of wealth and security dancing in their heads. They came to fulfill their dreams. And, even if great wealth was to elude them, there was the promise of a comfortable home in the suburbs, two cars in the garage, a good job, and an employer-paid pension plan that would allow them to relax and enjoy their retirement years, and to live happily ever after.

They held fast to that dream, which kept them going through thirty or forty years of work. Yet today, for many, that dream has turned into a nightmare, and life has become, in the words of the late, great African-American poet and author Langston Hughes, "a broken-winged bird that cannot fly."

THE FUNDING SHORTFALL

More and more companies, including some of the biggest names in corporate American history, are eliminating those pension plans, or freezing the benefits. In the early 1980s, more than 110,000 U.S. companies sponsored pension plans for their employees. Less than twenty years later, that number had fallen below 30,000, and those plans which are still in place are underfunded to the tune of nearly five hundred billion dollars—that's $500,000,000,000!

In the first four years of this century alone, nearly 20 percent of the companies on the Fortune 1000 list eliminated or froze their defined-benefit plans. Few, if any, of the major airlines now provide them, and such big names as Hewlett-Packard, IBM, Verizon, Motorola, Sears, and NCR Corp. are among the giant corporations which have either scrapped them or frozen them, or plan to do so. Some have filed bankruptcy as a way of getting out from under their "guaranteed" pension-fund obligations.

In that regard, perhaps the worst example is that of the Polaroid Corporation, which filed for bankruptcy in 2001. When the company was sold three and a half years later, the top two executives received a combined payout of more than $20 million, while several thousand Polaroid retirees received one-time payments of $47 each. Adding insult to injury, they also lost their life insurance and medical benefits.

Other companies, anxious to divest themselves of le-gitimately incurred pension obligations, have taken to fil-ing what are called "presumptive lawsuits" against their own retired employees. They begin by drastically and unilaterally cutting benefits, despite written agreements to the contrary. Then, anticipating lawsuits by disenfranchised retirees, they strike the first blow, filing a "complaint for declaratory judgment." They carefully select jurisdictions where judges are known to be pro-business and that are often far removed from where the affected retirees live. These companies make it as difficult as possible for their retirees to gain relief, leaving them scrambling to live on greatly reduced incomes.

> IF YOU'VE BEEN COUNTING ON THAT PENSION YOU'VE WORKED SO HARD FOR FOR ALL THESE YEARS—EXPECTING IT WOULD ALLOW YOU TO SPEND YOUR RETIREMENT YEARS IN COMFORT—THERE EXISTS THE POSSIBILITY THAT YOU'LL BE SERIOUSLY DISAPPOINTED.

Extreme cases? Perhaps so! But they might well serve as warning shots across your bow. If you've been counting on that pension you've worked so hard for all these years—expecting it would allow you to spend your retirement years in comfort—there exists the possibility that you'll be seriously disappointed.

PENSION RIGHTS CENTER

If you believe your pension rights are in jeopardy or have been violated, I suggest you contact the Pension Rights Center, based in Washington, D.C. Founded in 1976, it's the nation's only consumer organization dedicated solely to protecting and promoting the retirement security of American workers, retirees, and their families. To learn more about this organization and how it can help you, visit its website at www.pensionrights.org, or write to Pension Rights Center, 1350 Connecticut Avenue NW, Washington, D.C. 20036.

Government "Help"

But, you may be thinking, that's exactly why Congress passed that 1974 law which resulted in the formation of the Pension Benefit Guaranty Corporation (PBGC). Surely that will protect me if my employer defaults. Perhaps—and then again, perhaps not. Like so many other government programs, the PBGC is running a huge deficit, to the tune of more than $20 billion, and projections are that it may soon top $30 billion. Even in free-spending Washington, that's a whole lot of money.

Counting on government help is generally risky at best. Among those who have repeatedly sounded that warning is Milton Friedman, one of America's most respected economists. A former university professor, U.S. Treasury spokesman, and member of President Ronald Reagan's Economic Policy Advisory Board, he has received many honors during his long and distinguished career, including a Nobel Memorial Prize in Economics, the Presidential Medal of Freedom, and the National Medal of Science.

Friedman was never one to pull any punches about government programs. On one occasion he said, "Many people want the government to protect the consumer. A much more urgent problem is to protect the consumer from the government." Another time he remarked, "If you put the federal government in charge of the Sahara Desert, in five years there'd be a shortage of sand." President Reagan himself said it this way: "The most terrifying words in the English language are: 'I'm from the government and I'm here to help.'"

Be aware that the word "Guaranty" in PBGC isn't necessarily what that word implies. For example, even if that agency does take over when your employer defaults on paying its pension obligations, there's no assurance that you'll get the promised amount. In some cases, after the PBGC becomes the trustee of a defaulted plan, retirees receive significantly less than what had been promised originally.

On its website, www.pbgc.gov, the agency advises current retirees in regards to what they might expect: "If you are already receiving a pension, we will continue paying you without interruption during our review. These payments will be an **estimate** of the benefits that PBGC can pay under the insurance program, and they may be less than you were receiving from your plan."

With defined-benefit pension plans predicted to disappear within the next decade or so, and with the uncertainties about the future of Social Security, you could find yourself with a "shortage of sand" in your retirement bucket and facing the same situation your forebears faced a century ago—having sole responsibility for providing for your retirement years. And that isn't necessarily a bad thing.

> YOUR BEST APPROACH TO DEVELOPING LONG-RANGE SECURITY MAY WELL BE TO SEEK THE ADVICE OF A FINANCIAL PLANNING SPECIALIST WHO MAY HELP YOU REALIZE YOUR FINANCIAL GOALS

Our purpose in all this isn't to frighten you, but primarily to sound a wake-up call. As life expectancies keep climbing and government and corporate benefits continue to erode, your best approach to developing long-range security may well be to seek the advice of a financial planning specialist who may help you realize your financial goals.

As you begin, you'll find there are thousands of individuals, with widely varied levels of skills and experience, who describe themselves as financial planners. In a later chapter, we'll talk about how to identify those who are best qualified to meet your needs.

Chapter 7

Tax Traps—and How to Avoid Them!

As a taxpayer, you are required to be fully in compliance with the United States Tax Code, which is currently the size and weight of the Budweiser Clydesdales.

Dave Barry

Exaggeration is often used as a tool to generate laughter in order to make a point. Pulitzer Prize-winning columnist Dave Barry has long been a master at it, and the above statement strikes us as both funny and to the point. However, as we're about to see, it may not be that much of an exaggeration, after all.

Let's do some calculations. First, we have to know the actual size and weight of the U.S. tax code, then the size and weight of a Budweiser Clydesdale, and finally the number of Clydesdales Dave was including in his comparison.

The first step seems easy enough, doesn't it? After all, it's Congress that's in charge of writing it, so all we should have to do is ask a few members of that body just how big the tax code is, right? Well, not exactly! According to statements a number of them have made, they're not quite on the same page or even, in some cases, in the same area code.

To avoid embarrassing anyone, we won't name names, but their estimates as to the number of pages in the tax code range, with one exception, from 2,500 to 60,000, and the number of words from one million up to 500 million. Now, one might hope that those folks we've elected, who are in charge of levying taxes, would have a little better grasp of exactly what they've done to us, but things happen fast in Washington, and sometimes it's hard to keep up.

A Moving Target

Between 2001 and 2005, Congress made nearly 2,000 changes to the tax code, an average of three changes *every day* they were in session, and it's probably safe to say that few if any of those changes were in our favor. No wonder the troops are so confused!

To illustrate that last point, the editors of *Money* magazine pick one family's tax documents every year and send them to dozens of tax preparers. Invariably, they get dozens of different results.

If you happen to be among the millions of Americans who find our tax laws confusing and filling out our tax returns frustrating at best, don't feel bad about it. As eminent a genius as he was, Albert Einstein was in the same boat. He once said, "The hardest thing to understand in the world is the income tax," and he died more than half a century ago, long before the tax code acquired today's massive proportions.

Now, let's turn our attention to those Clydesdales. First of all, a fully grown Clydesdale (which, for those who may not watch Budweiser television commercials, is a very large horse) weighs between 2,000 and 2,300 pounds and is about six feet high at the shoulders. As it happens, Budweiser owns about 250 of them, but it seems unlikely that Barry had that number in mind. Budweiser generally features them in teams of eight, or a combined weight of eight to nine tons.

By the way, that one exception we mentioned above was a congressman who thought the tax code had 1.3 million pages. He didn't mention number of words but that's probably what he had in mind. The tax code has nowhere that number of pages—yet—but if it did, Barry's estimate wouldn't have been so far off after all. According to the highly respected Cato Institute, the actual number of pages, as of 2006, is 66,498, up from 40,500 a decade earlier.

Not only do the rules and regulations change and increase regularly, but the percentage of our income taken from us by federal, state, and local governments each year continues to grow. For example, from 1990 to 2000, it grew from 30.5 percent to 33.6 percent. No wonder planning for our financial independence today, next year, and in the years to come can be so uncertain and so difficult. That's why it's so important to develop long-range strategies that can minimize our own tax burdens, and those of our heirs—and their heirs, as well.

Our nation's first income tax law was passed by Congress in 1862. It was abolished in 1872 and reinstated in 1894, lasting only one year before the U.S. Supreme Court ruled it unconstitutional. (No wonder they were called "the good old days.") Income taxes became a permanent fixture in 1913 with the passage of the sixteenth amendment to the constitution. Today, the IRS has about twice the budget of the FBI, and eight times as many employees.

EXCHANGING ONE HEADACHE FOR ANOTHER

Given the ever growing complexities of preparing income tax returns, growing numbers of Americans turn to professional tax preparers for help. Twenty years ago, fewer than half did so, but today the number has grown to 60 percent or more. Naturally, the growing demand has resulted in significant increases in the number of professional tax preparers. With no specific training required or regulatory system in place, that field is wide open to just about anyone who wishes to claim that title.

As I've already described, the world of taxes is incredibly complex, making it difficult for even the best professionals to stay up to speed. For example, in the past six years, the number of IRS tax forms has increased from 475 to 582; and in the past decade, 26,000 pages have been added to the federal tax rules and regulations, causing the cost of compliance for federal taxpayers to more than double to an estimated $265 billion.

> BE AWARE THAT, EVEN THOUGH YOUR TAX RETURN MAY BE SIGNED BY A THIRD-PARTY PREPARER, THE RESPONSIBILITY FOR ITS ACCURACY IS SQUARELY ON YOUR SHOULDERS, AND THE PENALTIES FOR ERRORS CAN BE SUBSTANTIAL.

If you decide you need a professional to prepare your tax returns, choose carefully. Keeping abreast of the enormous complexities of the tax code, plus the never-ending changes in the rules and regulations, is no easy task, even for a professional. Be aware that, even though your tax return may be signed by a third-party preparer, the responsibility for its accuracy is squarely on your shoulders, and the penalties for errors can be substantial.

Feathering the Government's Nest

It was the late French statesman J.B. Colbert who is credited as having said, "The art of taxation consists in so plucking the goose as to obtain the largest amount of feathers with the least possible amount of hissing."

Congress and the Internal Revenue Service have long since perfected the "plucking the goose" part, without paying a whole lot of attention to how much hissing it triggers on the part of those being plucked.

In 2006, the plucking amounted to an average of $20,044 from every family in America, and that's just by the federal government. By the time state and local governments get into the act, nearly one-third of your annual income will have disappeared.

One thing that continually puzzles me is why so many taxpayers actually do some of the plucking themselves, by having more of their hard-earned dollars withheld from their paychecks than is necessary. Every year, the IRS refunds billions of dollars to taxpayers, with the average refund amounting to more than $2,400. Those billions of dollars represent interest-free loans to the government, which makes absolutely no sense.

> A WELL-QUALIFIED FINANCIAL PLANNER MAY COME TO YOUR RESCUE, POTENTIALLY SAVING A LARGE QUANTITY OF YOUR FINANCIAL FEATHERS AND SIGNIFICANTLY REDUCING, IF NOT ELIMINATING, THE PLUCKING, AND THUS THE NEED FOR YOU TO HISS.

As the overwhelming majority of American taxpayers realize, our increasingly complex system of paying taxes is badly in need of major reform. Yet, until the day that happens, we're very much at the mercy of fiscally irresponsible, big-spending politicians.

That's where a well-qualified financial planner may come to your rescue, potentially saving a large quantity of your financial feathers and significantly reducing, if not eliminating, the plucking, and thus the need for you to hiss.

WHERE TO BEGIN

An important starting point in tax planning is your income tax return. If any financial advisor you talk to doesn't ask to see your return, right at the start, *don't*, under any circumstances, offer to provide it. Instead, grab your hat and run. If you're not wearing a hat, just run. In my view, failure to ask that question automatically disqualifies that individual as a competent advisor.

Your tax return is one of the key tools a qualified advisor needs to study in order to determine where you currently are and to begin structuring a sound plan for you. It allows your advisor to guide you through the complicated and ever-changing maze of tax laws, avoiding the pitfalls that await the unwary, allowing you to retain a greater share of the assets you've worked so hard to accumulate and to pass them along to your designated beneficiaries.

> YOUR TAX RETURN IS ONE OF THE KEY TOOLS A QUALIFIED ADVISOR NEEDS TO STUDY IN ORDER TO DETERMINE WHERE YOU CURRENTLY ARE AND TO BEGIN STRUCTURING A SOUND PLAN FOR YOU.

I can't say it strongly enough—if you're not asked to

provide a copy of your current tax return, you're talking to the wrong person! He or she can't build a sound structure without the foundation in place. It's like trying to hit a moving target in the dark, while wearing a blindfold. As the old saying goes, "aim at nothing and you'll hit it—every time!"

CHAPTER 8

SOME PROBLEMS WITH PROBATE

The only authentic evidence…which we have of the
survival of life after death is the ability of the judges
to read the intention of the testator long after he
has been buried.

FREDERICK E. CRANE

Frederick Crane was an attorney who served for many years as a judge in various New York courts during the early part of the twentieth century. He made the above comment, perhaps in jest or with tongue in cheek, during a speech before the New York State Bar Association in 1931. Nevertheless, the fact remains that in judicial proceedings, especially during the probate process, judges are often placed in the position of determining how the assets of a decedent's estate are to be distributed, even "long after he [or she] has been buried."

In *Merriam-Webster's Collegiate Dictionary*, 11th Edition, probate is defined as "the action or process of proving before a competent judicial authority that a document offered as official recognition and registration as the last will and testament of a deceased person is genuine."

With the guidance of a qualified financial advisor and an experienced estate planning attorney, the need to submit to the probate process may be eliminated. When an estate must go through probate, it can be very time-consuming and expensive, resulting not only in needless delays in settling the estate and distributing its assets, but in major tax consequences that could have been eliminated had probate been avoided.

Having already suffered the loss of a loved one, the probate experience—often extending over several months or, in some cases, for more than a year—can be a traumatic one for a surviving spouse and other loved ones. That's especially true when the surviving spouse and other heirs have no other sources of income and are in urgent need of funds which, with proper planning, could have been readily available but instead are locked up indefinitely as the probate process drags on and on. And, when the funds finally do become available, they've been reduced by court costs and attorney fees.

JOINT OWNERSHIP PITFALLS

In an effort to avoid probate, many people, typically married couples, place their assets in joint ownership, usually as "Joint Tenants with Right of Survivorship" (JTWROS). When one of them dies, ownership of these assets passes automatically to the survivor, with no need for probate.

One potential problem that can arise, however, is if both parties die simultaneously, or if one dies shortly after the other, before any changes are made regarding the disposition of the first person's estate. To prevent such an occurrence, a competent advisor will make certain to take appropriate and immediate action upon the death of a client.

Another potential pitfall involves the naming of beneficiaries. Most people tend to choose a spouse as primary beneficiary, with children as secondary (or contingent) beneficiaries. If the primary beneficiary dies before the owner, the secondary ones move up to the primary position. In such cases, however, the unexpected death of one of these secondary beneficiaries could have consequences which the owner never intended.

Yet another pitfall may result in the case of a single person who has sole ownership of a significant amount of assets and wishes to avoid probate by naming a joint owner who would otherwise have no claim on his estate. Such a move can backfire, however, if the co-owner pledges his share as collateral for a loan, or if it's attached by creditors. And, when the original owner dies, the co-owner may claim the jointly owned property, disinheriting the rightful heirs.

A qualified financial advisor can help clients properly establish joint ownership accounts while avoiding the pitfalls which we've described.

THE IMPORTANCE OF TRUSTS

Properly drawn trusts are extremely important tools which can be legally set up to avoid probate, even over several generations. This is especially important in the case of Individual Retirement Accounts

> IN DOING ESTATE PLANNING, IT'S IMPORTANT FOR THE OWNER TO THINK LIKE A PARENT.

(IRAs), which dictate the number of years over which funds must be withdrawn. By structuring what's known as a "Stretch IRA," withdrawal of the funds accumulated in an IRA can be "stretched" over the life expectancy of the beneficiary, a child, or even a grandchild, thus lengthening the number of years over which withdrawals are required.

Trust documents should be prepared by an attorney who specializes in that field. The problem with a "do-it-yourself" trust is that its faults won't be discovered until after the owner's death, when it's too late to correct them.

In doing estate planning, it's important for the owner to think like a parent. The goal should be to make certain everything is handled after your death as you'd handle it if you were still alive. Where there are multiple beneficiaries (children, for example), this can be very complex. A good advisor will establish separate accounts for each child, which may help avoid disputes among the heirs and, in turn, the heirs of the heirs.

> A QUALIFIED FINANCIAL PLANNER MAY BE ABLE TO HELP YOU AND YOUR HEIRS AVOID THE KINDS OF LEGAL ENTANGLEMENTS, HEAVY EXPENSES, AND LONG DELAYS THAT COULD HAVE BEEN AVOIDED BY PROPER ESTATE PLANNING

A qualified financial planner may be able to help you and your heirs avoid the kinds of legal entanglements, heavy expenses, and long delays that could have been avoided by proper estate planning. Sadly, disputes over the assumed, but not clearly stated, intentions of the deceased person can cause bitter and long-lasting disruptions of family relationships—disruptions which could have been avoided.

PART TWO

HOW TO FIND THE RIGHT FINANCIAL ADVISOR

Chapter 9

Finding the Right Planner

Set your expectations high; find men and women whose integrity and values you respect; get their agreement on a course of action; and give them your ultimate trust.

John Akers

With millions of Americans, primarily the baby boomer generation (those born between 1946 and 1964), getting closer and closer to retirement, if they're not already there, it's not at all surprising to see a sharp increase in the number of those who regard financial planning for retirees as a fertile field. Here, they hope to sow the seeds that will blossom into products and services designed to meet the needs of the burgeoning senior market and thus, hopefully, to harvest great rewards.

It's estimated that the 78 million boomers who will be joining the ranks of the retired in the coming years will have a combined total of more than $8 trillion to invest, not counting the enor-

> OVER THE NEXT HALF-CENTURY, IT'S PROJECTED THAT $41 TRILLION WILL CHANGE HANDS, MAKING IT THE LARGEST INTERGENERATIONAL TRANSFER OF WEALTH IN U.S. HISTORY.

mous sums they're projected to inherit. Over the next half-century, it's projected that $41 trillion will change hands, making it the largest intergenerational transfer of wealth in U.S. history. Not all of it, of course, will find its way into the pockets and bank accounts of the boomer generation.

Nevertheless, enormous sums of money are involved, and financial planning certainly ranks among the highest needs and greatest concerns of the baby boomer generation. Thus it follows, as the night the day, that newly-minted "senior" advisors are popping up everywhere, joining the ranks of those planners who have simply tacked the S-word onto whatever designation they were already using—whether it be clergyman (or woman), insurance agent, social worker, realtor, doctor, lawyer, Indian chief, or, yes, even funeral director. As the late, great comic Jimmy Durante used to mutter in mock dismay: "Everybody wants to get into the act."

That's *not* to suggest that those who use the word "senior" in their titles do so simply as a marketing tactic, or lack the

> *ALWAYS* LOOK BEYOND AND BEHIND WHATEVER TITLE A FINANCIAL PLANNER MAY USE, OR WHATEVER LEVEL OF EXPERTISE HE OR SHE MAY CLAIM TO HAVE.

qualifications to render qualified and ethical services to their clients. In fact, there are many highly qualified financial planners serving the senior community. Rather, consider it merely as a warning to *always* look beyond and behind whatever title a financial planner may use, or whatever level of expertise he or she may claim to have.

ON SHAKY GROUND

The majority of Americans who are nearing retirement are woefully unprepared financially for the future. According to the Employee Benefit Research Institute's 2006 Retirement Survey, 52 percent of American workers, ages fifty-five and older, have less than $50,000 saved toward retirement. And, in the best-selling book, *Who's Watching Your Money, The 17 Paladin Principles for Selecting a Financial Advisor*, author Jack Waymire writes: "Baby boomers are turning [sixty], and the vast majority of them are facing uncertain financial futures. It is well past time to start thinking about retirement."

Given the uncertainties surrounding company pension plans and the future of Social Security, those who have been counting on them to meet their needs may be on shaky ground.

Accordingly, choosing a qualified financial advisor to help you chart your course may be extremely important. The key word, of course, is "qualified." As we saw in an earlier chapter, those practicing in this field come equipped with a bewildering array of titles and designations.

Unfortunately, virtually anyone can describe himself or herself as a financial planner—or some variation on that theme—so that offers absolutely no assurance of qualifications, experience, or reputation. While some of those names are especially significant, others may be virtually meaningless. Placing your financial future in the hands of someone based primarily on a self-conferred title, or on the set of initials following his or her name, or simply on a pleasing personality, is a risky proposition at best.

As is true with virtually every major decision or choice you make, doing your homework is extremely important. In the long run, the planner you choose will likely have as big an impact on your fiscal well-being as your doctor has on your physical well-being, so be sure to use as much care in choosing one as you do in selecting your doctor, accountant, attorney, or any other professional.

THE EVALUATION PROCESS

Begin by following the advice from business executive John Akers, which appears at the start of this chapter: "Find men and women whose integrity and values you respect." Without integrity, every other qualification an advisor or planner has will be meaningless. Often, as is the case in choosing any professional, a referral from someone you know and trust may be sufficient. However, keep in mind that the term "financial planner" has absolutely no legal standing—it can be used by anyone!

> IN THE LONG RUN, THE PLANNER YOU CHOOSE WILL LIKELY HAVE AS BIG AN IMPACT ON YOUR FISCAL WELL-BEING AS YOUR DOCTOR HAS ON YOUR PHYSICAL WELL-BEING.

So, it's extremely important to do your homework. You can get a good handle on a planner's qualifications and integrity by asking the following questions:

- How long have you been in business?
- What professional credentials/designations do you hold?
- How many clients do you have?
- May I contact a few of them as references?
- Have you ever been disciplined in the course of your business for any inappropriate or illegal actions?

Once you've satisfied yourself on the integrity issue, you can move on to the next steps in the process. At this point, you've probably identified one or two individuals with whom you felt "connected" or "comfortable," so a very important question to ask them is: "Who in your firm will work with me?" That individual with whom you feel some rapport may be the firm's principal, who'll sign you up and then turn you over to someone in the firm you've never met.

That's not necessarily a bad thing, unless that principal you felt comfortable with will no longer be available to you. Be sure the relationship process is clearly explained before you sign on the dotted line. For example, I have excellent and well-trained staff members who handle many of the details on my clients' accounts. Every day, we get dozens of calls from clients, on almost anything that involves their finances: "What do you recommend I do with my CD which is maturing next month?" Or: "I'm getting ready to buy a new car. Should I pay cash, or finance it?"

I couldn't be doing the best job for my clients if I had to field every call, every inquiry. Having staff members handle the details frees me up to keep close watch on industry trends and regulations which may impact our clients' accounts. I'm able to focus on the broad picture while they handle the day-to-day operations. At the same time, I make it clear to my clients that I'm always available and accessible to them.

Another important consideration is accountability. While staff members may handle routine matters, the advisor you choose should meet with you regularly to review your portfolio and keep you up-to-date on its status. I make it a point to personally meet with each client periodically, and before that meeting ends, we make an appointment for the next one. You should expect no less from your financial planner.

During the interview process, make careful note of how well the prospective advisor *listens* to you. The late George C. Marshall, U.S. Army Chief of Staff during World War II and later U.S. Secretary of State, had this three-part formula for listening: "Listen to the other person's story; listen to the other person's full story; listen to the other person's full story first."

That's good advice. If the advisors you interview are so busy trying to impress you with tales of their knowledge and experience, instead of listening to you and learning what your goals and objectives are, it's probably a good idea to look elsewhere.

Be sure to ask the advisors about their specialty, or niche. An advisor who primarily works with younger people or small businesses is probably not the best fit for retirees, or those who are planning to take that step. And the size of the average portfolio they handle is another important consideration. For example, if the advisor's typical client is extremely wealthy and you aren't, or vice versa, that's not likely to be the ideal match.

> YOU'D BE WISE TO AVOID PLANNERS WHO CLAIM TO BE ALL THINGS TO ALL PEOPLE; THE FIELD IS SO COMPLEX THAT THE PERSON WHO CLAIMS TO BE A ONE-MAN BAND IS PROBABLY OUT OF TUNE, AND CERTAINLY OUT OF TOUCH.

You'd be wise to avoid planners who claim to be all things to all people; the field is so complex that the person who claims to be a one-man band is probably out of tune, and certainly out of touch. My client base is comprised of those who are approaching retirement or have already retired. In order to give them the very best service and advice, I work closely with tax accountants, attorneys, and others who are far more qualified than I am in their respective fields.

DECODING THE CREDENTIALS

Learning what credentials an advisor holds and what those credentials mean is also an important part of the selection process. The most significant designations include, but are not limited to, Certified Financial Planner (CFP), issued by the Certified Financial Planner Board of Standards, Inc.; Personal Financial Specialist (PFS), issued by the American Institute of Certified Public Accountants; and Chartered Financial Consultant (ChFC), issued by The American College (formerly The American College of Life Underwriters).

The requirements for earning the CFP designation include: a bachelor's degree (as of January 2007); passing the CFP Certification Examination, which is a three-session, ten-hour exam covering every aspect of financial planning; three years of qualifying full-time work experience; adherence to the CFP Board of Standards' Code of Ethics and Professional Responsibility; and passing a background check.

The right to use the CFP designation is by no means a lifetime one. Instead, it must be renewed every two years. The process includes: completion of a detailed renewal application; disclosure of any investigations or legal proceedings that apply to business or professional conduct; determination by the CFP Board of Standards of ongoing compliance with its ethical standards; and satisfactory completion of 30 hours of continuing education.

Those holding the PFS and certain other certifications are subject to similar requirements. At the other end of the spectrum are those who may have simply completed a brief self-study course and who are subject to no certification requirements and use self-conferred titles.

Before entrusting your financial future to any advisor, you'd do well to visit the website of the National Association of Securities Dealers (NASD), which lists more than sixty professional designations used by financial advisors, analysts, auditors, consultants, counselors, managers, planners, practitioners, specialists, and stockbrokers, who may or may not be accredited, certified, chartered, qualified, or registered. Shown in alphabetical order by their initials, they run the gamut from AAMS (Accredited Asset Management Specialist) to WMS (Wealth Management Specialist).

To access the list, go to www.nasd.org, click on "Investor Information," then "Investor Protection," then "Understanding Professional Designations," where you'll find a box labeled "View all designations in a printer-friendly format." Each of the dozens of listings includes: the name and website address of the issuing organization; the initial experience and education requirements; the ongoing experience and education requirements; the investor complaint and disciplinary processes, if any; and the ability to check the individual's status online.

With the integrity and qualifications of prospective advisors established, the next step is to determine the areas in which they specialize and which are best suited to your needs, which may range from asset management, estate planning, retirement issues, tax counseling, investment advice, or other aspects of financial planning.

Advisor Compensation

At this point, a key question to ask is: "How are you paid?" Here, again, you'll find a broad range. Some are salaried employees of their firm; some are paid fees based on an hourly rate or on a percentage of the assets being managed; some are on commission, based on the financial products they sell; and some earn a combination of fees and commissions.

A problem inherent in commission arrangements is possible conflicts of interest. If the advisors you're considering sell insurance products, securities, mutual funds, or any other instruments on which they receive commissions, they obviously depend, to a degree, on the providers of those products.

That doesn't necessarily rule out such products. Some investment products on which commissions are paid are a good fit in certain situations. When the planner recommends such products to you, you should be made aware that commissions are involved, and be certain that the planner isn't being paid both commissions and fees on the same transactions. And, when you're shown the projected returns on a recommended investment, it's always wise to ask if that return is net of all costs and fees.

A word of caution: a prospective client told me recently that one advisor had asked for an up-front fee of $20,000. Under no circumstances should you pay any fees in advance. Also, before putting money into a recommended investment, find out what penalties (also called back-end fees) might be involved should you need to make withdrawals on certain products, including annuities and some mutual funds, prior to maturity.

INTERNET TOOLS

To help you make the most informed choice, and the one that best suits your needs, there are some tools available on the Internet which we highly recommend.

First, visit the website of the Certified Financial Planner Board of Standards, Inc. at www.cfp.net. On the home page, click on "How to Choose a Planner." Then, on the drop-down menu, click on "Interviewing Checklist," which is a series of questions designed to help you evaluate the qualifications of the candidates you're considering.

Also, visit the website of the National Association of Personal Financial Advisors at www.napfa.org. On the home page, click on "Public," and then on "Comprehensive Financial Planning Checklist," which is a document listing service offered; method of providing services; educational background, certifications; experience; compensation; and regulatory matters.

The next step on the same site is to click again on "Public," and then on "Comprehensive Financial Planning Diagnostic," a detailed, twenty-five question tool covering every aspect of the advisor's background and method of operation. Following the list of questions is an "Answer Key," outlining the most appropriate responses to each of them.

Armed with these tools, and coupled with your personal impressions, you'll be well equipped to select the financial planner best suited to meet your current and long-term needs.

The Top Ten

In the tradition made famous by David Letterman on the CBS Late Show, but in a more serious vein, we'll conclude by presenting our own Top Ten list—a summary of the ten most important tests you should use in deciding on the financial planner who's right for you.

1. ***Your Tax Return***: It's one of the key tools a qualified advisor needs to study in order to determine where you currently are and to begin structuring a sound plan for you. If you're not asked for it, you're talking to the wrong person.

2. ***Financial Physical***: Just as a doctor can't diagnose an ailment and prescribe a solution without asking the proper questions and doing an intense exam, a good financial advisor can't make a proper recommendation without having all the pertinent information.

3. ***Estate Planning/Account Titling***: If the advisor you're interviewing is creative, and your estate isn't complex, all of your assets may be passed outside of probate.

4. ***Beneficiary Designations***: Properly recording the ownership of assets (joint tenancy, for example) and designating beneficiaries are both extremely important, both for minimizing taxes and to make certain that no beneficiaries are inadvertently disinherited.

5. ***Accountability/Reviews***: The advisor you choose should meet with you regularly to review your portfolio and keep you up-to-date on its status. I meet personally with each client periodically, and before that meeting ends, we make an appointment for the next one.

6. Staff/Associates: A capable and well-trained staff can handle many of the details involving client accounts, allowing the advisor to keep close watch on industry trends and regulations which may impact those accounts, and to focus on the broad picture while others handle the day-to-day operations.

7. Fees vs. Commissions: Advisors are paid in a variety of ways, including fees, commissions, or a combination thereof. You should always be made aware of what commissions, if any, the advisor would receive on the investment products he or she recommends.

8. Product Costs and Penalties: These should not be the biggest deciding factor in choosing a product. However, you should know what they are and agree to them.

9. References: Before doing business with an advisor, obtain the names of several of that advisor's clients whose circumstances are similar to yours, and be sure to check with them for references.

10. Qualifications/Experience: Learning what credentials an advisor holds and what those credentials mean is very important. The most significant designations include Certified Financial Planner (CFP), Personal Financial Specialist (PFS), and Chartered Financial Consultant (ChFC).

In the following chapters, I'll expand on the above Ten Tests. I don't believe the public is "armed" enough when they venture out to try to find that one person, or team of people, who will help them work toward their financial independence. By using these tests every time you interview a potential financial advisor, you may lessen the risk of working with the wrong person for your situation. By being knowledgeable about what the financial planning industry is all about, you will build that "suit of armor" you will need to help you eliminate the salesman and find the professional.

CHAPTER 10

TEST #1: TAX RETURNS

The United States is the only country where it takes more brains to figure your tax than to earn the money to pay it.

EDWARD J. GURNEY

Trying to provide competent financial advice and guidance to a client without all the pertinent data is like trying to complete a jigsaw puzzle with some of the pieces missing. In order to make a proper recommendation, a planner has to look at the entire financial picture, and the tax return is a very important piece of the puzzle. The advisor can immediately see what tax bracket you're in, which can help to determine whether your portfolio can benefit from "tax efficient investments" when possible.

One example may be diversifying your investments to include "tax-deferred" investment products, such as annuities, which may generate earnings without increasing your taxable income or your tax liability. If the return shows you're being taxed on your Social Security benefits, this strategy may also reduce the tax liability on that part of your income.

Your tax bracket may lead the advisor to recommend tax-free municipal bonds or bond funds where the interest and dividends earned are not taxable. On the other hand, your return may show that you have too much tax-free income, which adds to the taxability of your Social Security benefits.

Your tax return will also indicate whether or not you should take advantage of contributing to—or increasing contributions to—a company-sponsored retirement

> YOUR RETURN MAY SHOW THAT YOU HAVE TOO MUCH TAX-FREE INCOME, WHICH ADDS TO THE TAXABILITY OF YOUR SOCIAL SECURITY BENEFITS.

plan or an Individual Retirement Account (IRA). This could kill two birds with one stone: possibly giving you a tax deduction, while saving more money toward your retirement to supplement pension and Social Security income.

CASES IN POINT

I once reviewed a potential client's tax return after he told me he'd been retired for four years but continued to contribute to his IRA. I noticed there was no earned income from a W-2 or self-employment and informed him he was *not* allowed to add to his IRA without it. He said his accountant told him he could as long as he didn't deduct it on his taxes. The accountant was wrong. You must have an earned income to contribute, regardless of whether you deduct it or not. The penalty for over-contributing to an IRA is 6 percent for every year it remains there. Of course, I recommended he remove the excess contribution.

Another client told me he'd been contributing to a Simplified Employee Pension Plan (SEPP) for the past ten years. As I reviewed the current tax return, I noticed there was no deduction for the SEPP and asked the client if he had contributed to it that year. He said he had. I proceeded to call the tax preparer who did the return and asked him why it wasn't showing as a deduction and he told me that the client didn't tell him about it. I was surprised that this tax advisor, who had done this return for ten years, didn't ask his client if he had contributed to his SEPP that year. Had I not asked for the tax return, this client would have missed out on a big deduction that year.

Several years ago, I met with a client who had just turned seventy-three. As I reviewed the tax return, I noticed there were no IRA withdrawals added to the taxable income. The client said she didn't need the money so she is leaving it for her children. The IRS Required Minimum Distribution Rules (RMD) require anyone reaching the age of 70.5 to start taking withdrawals from their IRAs. Neither her current financial advisor nor her tax preparer informed her of this rule. The IRS penalty for not withdrawing the RMD is 50 percent of the amount not withdrawn. That means if you're supposed to take out $5,000 and you don't, it will cost you $2,500 in penalties.

> IT'S IMPERATIVE THAT AN ADVISOR BE WELL-VERSED IN HOW TO READ A TAX RETURN, IN ORDER TO BE ABLE TO CATCH THESE AND OTHER EASILY MADE MISTAKES.

It's imperative that an advisor be well-versed in how to read a tax return, in order to be able to catch these and other easily made mistakes. They may help keep you from paying more in taxes than you should and avoid high IRS penalties.

A financial planner who's experienced with tax returns can also determine whether you're having too much tax withheld, so you can stop giving the government an interest-free loan from your hard-earned money, and instead have it work for you. Conversely, the planner can determine if you don't have enough tax withheld, which may be causing you to pay estimated tax payments or possibly tax penalties.

One of the biggest culprits for underpayment of taxes is Social Security. Most people don't have taxes withheld from their Social Security. Many times, I recommend they have taxes withheld by going to www.irs.gov and filling out the form, or calling their local Social Security office. By looking at their return, I can advise them what percentage to have withheld.

I've had many clients question why I ask them to bring their personal tax returns in with their other important papers. I hope the above explanations make it very clear why you do *not* want to work with an advisor who fails to ask for your tax return. I could write a whole book on the tax issues I've come across in reviewing tax returns. One of the most annoying issues to me involves clients who are no longer required to file a return because their income isn't high enough, but their tax preparer keeps charging them to file one.

My clients are also required to bring in their tax returns annually, so I can determine if our plan of action is working, or whether changes should be made. I constantly have clients asking me tax questions, which I can easily answer because I have their most current return on file. Only a competent advisor goes to this extent.

Remember, this is a test. Do *not* offer to provide your tax return if the advisor doesn't ask for it. You need to work with an advisor who knows the importance of making recommendations based on your entire financial picture, and can advise you on what the tax consequences will be in implementing those recommendations.

Chapter 11

TEST #2: The Financial Physical

Money is better than poverty, if only for financial reasons.

Just as a doctor can't diagnose an ailment and prescribe a solution without asking the proper questions and doing an intense exam, a good financial advisor can't make a proper recommendation without having all the pertinent information. I call this the "Financial Physical."

The financial advisors you're considering should ask you to bring to your initial interview, not only your current tax return, but all your current investment statements. That includes mutual funds and brokerage account statements, IRA and other retirement statements, pension statements and Social Security statements, if applicable, annuity and insurance policy statements and/or contracts, and any long-term-care policies you may have. Most year-end statements arc advantageous because they may show beginning of year values and current values, so the advisor can determine recent dividend history and growth performance.

I also have my potential clients fill out a confidential "Financial Physical Data Form" which I provide for them. This will list personal information, bank accounts, investments, insurances, real estate, and other assets. On a separate form, also provided for them, they'll list household income and expenses for monthly and/or annual cash flow. This will help me to determine how much income they need to stay in the lifestyle they're accustomed to.

These forms ask them questions about their primary financial concerns and how they'd improve their financial situation if they could (60 percent of the time I get the answer "win the lottery" on that last question, showing me the client has a sense of humor, which I appreciate).

I know this requires some homework on their part, but when they come in for their Financial Physical, I want to be able to sit down and talk to them about their past investing experience, and what their retirement dreams and goals are, without having to take a lot of time to fill out the data forms myself. As I go through the forms with the potential client, I add a lot of my own notes to them.

Based on all this information, I can easily see if they're on track to accomplish those goals, or whether I'd recommend changes in order to make the journey a little smoother. I also promise them that if I see they're already doing the right thing, I'll be the first person to tell them.

CASES IN POINT

A couple who had attended one of my public seminars several years ago set up an appointment to meet with me to do their Financial Physical. They came in with their "homework" done, and brought all the appropriate statements and their tax return. After going through the data form with them and reviewing their current investment strategy, I determined they had very good mutual funds and there wasn't much I'd do differently. I asked them to call me if their situation changed, and I'd be glad to help them.

Four months later, they called to tell me they'd just won a *10-million-dollar* lottery. At first, I thought they were kidding, but quickly determined they were very serious. They drove straight to my office, from the lottery office, because they didn't want to hold on to such a large (to say the least) check. I still have a copy of that check in their file. The moral of this story is that if you do the right thing for the client, it will always come back to you!

I had another potential client tell me she was going to be seventy and a half, so I told her how much she'd have to take out of her IRA accounts under the required minimum distribution rules. She said she didn't need that income and wasn't happy about paying taxes on money she didn't need. After studying her entire situation, I was able to recommend that she stop taking income from her taxable investments and move the taxable money to a tax-deferred annuity, letting that grow for the kids.

The income she'll have to take from her IRA will replace the previous income. This way, instead of adding additional income to her tax return, her income will stay the same; it's just coming from another place. Good advisors can be very creative after they have all the pertinent information to make proper recommendations for your particular situation.

THE NEXT STEP

After the initial meeting, and with complete financial information at my fingertips, I can prepare for the next appointment, which is when I make specific recommendations. By analyzing the clients' situation, and having the actual monthly or quarterly statements, I can get the exact names of mutual funds (several funds with some fund families sound very similar), stocks, bonds, and types of annuities or insurance policies they have, and if they're all working hand-in-hand to help the clients reach their goals.

> IF THE ADVISOR IS MORE INTERESTED IN TALKING ABOUT THE WEATHER, SHOWING YOU PICTURES OF HIS DOG, OR DISCUSSING THE LATEST FOOTBALL GAME WITH YOUR SPOUSE, THEN THEY ARE MORE LIKELY A PRODUCT SALESMAN THAN A FINANCIAL COUNSELOR.

I can get information directly from the statements, if clients aren't able to give me an answer I need, or if they have trouble understanding them, especially brokerage and annuity accounts. This allows me to do the proper research and gather performance data about their existing investments to go over with them at our next meeting.

It's imperative that a good advisor look at the entire financial picture before making a recommendation, to make sure he or she isn't duplicating what you already have, find areas that aren't helping you reach your goals, and make sure all your investments are working together to get you where you need to be.

Remember, this is another test! Do *not* offer to bring in any information you haven't been asked to provide. If the advisor is more interested in talking about the weather, showing you pictures of his dog, or discussing the latest football game with your spouse, then they are more likely a product salesman than a financial counselor.

As a little side test, make sure both spouses are present during these interviews, and make sure the advisor is addressing both of you. This will prevent you from working with someone who may be a bit chauvinistic. Both of you must have a good rapport with him or her in the event one of you becomes ill or passes away.

One couple told me their current advisor always talks to the husband and never addresses the wife. She said that's why she's looking for another advisor, since she's the one who handles the money!

Chapter 12

TEST #3:
Estate Planning/Account Titling

Good things happen only when planned. Bad things happen on their own.

Philip B. Crosby

As Benjamin Franklin said so famously more than two centuries ago, "In this world nothing can be said to be certain, except for death and taxes." In light of those certainties, a competent financial advisor should be well-versed in estate planning, account titling, and beneficiary designations.

We already covered the importance of the potential advisor being able to understand a tax return, but is he or she also bringing up concerns about how your assets will be handled if you should become ill or disabled, or how they'll pass to your spouse and ultimately to your children upon your death?

The advisor you're interviewing should be asking you questions about long-term care provisions, health insurance coverage, and living wills (also known as Health Care Proxies), which make your wishes clear regarding life-prolonging decisions.

A good advisor should ask questions about your family, especially children and grandchildren, to determine if your current will or estate plan will distribute the assets the way you think they will. In order to do this, they will have to have copies of your legal documents.

If you don't have a will, or haven't inquired about whether you need more extensive trust planning done, the advisor should be able to steer you in the right direction, based on the information you provided in the initial interview. He or she should be able to recommend a competent estate planning attorney for this part of the overall picture.

> A GOOD ADVISOR SHOULD ASK QUESTIONS ABOUT YOUR FAMILY, ESPECIALLY CHILDREN AND GRANDCHILDREN, TO DETERMINE IF YOUR CURRENT WILL OR ESTATE PLAN WILL DISTRIBUTE THE ASSETS THE WAY YOU THINK THEY WILL.

By reviewing your current statements, the advisor can see how they're titled. Most married couples have their non-retirement accounts titled as Joint Tenants with Right of Survivorship (JTWROS). This means if one spouse passes away, the surviving spouse has access to the account without having to go through probate. You want to try to avoid probate between spouses whenever possible.

I often see couples who have a checking account, investment account, or stock certificate titled in one spouse's name (which means their current advisor didn't care what would happen upon the death of that spouse). If that spouse passes away, the surviving spouse has no authority to sign on that account and must attain a form called "Letters Testamentary" from a court proceeding (called probate) stating that he or she is the deceased spouse's representative (also known as executor).

In my view, it's unthinkable to make a spouse have to go through the probate process, especially if it's just for one small account, when it could have easily been avoided by an advisor's recommendation to change the title.

CASE IN POINT

A very nice couple came to one of my public seminars and set up an appointment to meet with me for their financial physical. Between the time of the seminar and the appointment, the husband passed away. The wife eventually came in for an appointment and brought all the pertinent information. I found they had bank accounts in the husband's name only, a mutual fund statement that was jointly owned by her husband and his deceased sister, and annuities with their children as primary beneficiaries.

The cash flow statement we did showed that this spouse needed every dime of these assets to live on. She had to go to probate to have access to them (which took nine months), needed to get a death certificate on her husband's sister, and had to have their children liquidate the money from the annuity and give it back to her, causing them to pay taxes on it. What a mess! This could have been totally avoided if the previous "advisor" had been experienced in titling accounts properly.

> IF THE ADVISOR YOU'RE INTERVIEWING IS CREATIVE, AND YOUR ESTATE ISN'T COMPLEX, ALL OF YOUR ASSETS CAN BE PASSED OUTSIDE OF PROBATE, JUST BY TITLING THE ACCOUNTS PROPERLY.

If the advisor you're interviewing is creative, and your estate isn't complex, all of your assets can be passed outside of probate, not only to your spouse but to your children and grandchildren, just by titling the accounts properly. If the advisor brings up terms like Transfer On Death (TOD), Payable On Death (POD), or In Trust For (ITF—used mostly by banks on checking and savings accounts), then chances are you're talking to a very competent individual.

One example would be to suggest that you title the appropriate accounts as follows: Mr. John Doe and Mrs. Mary Doe, POD to Paul Doe and Susan Doe (the two children). In this case, if one spouse passes away, the account will belong to the surviving spouse. When the surviving spouse passes away, the account will automatically be divided between the children. This happens without a probate proceeding. The children should just have to produce death certificates and fill out the proper paperwork.

If you have an account you don't want to own jointly with your spouse for one reason or another, you can still add the TOD or POD option with your spouse's name if you want the account to go to him/her upon your death. While you're alive, the account is solely yours. Upon your death, it automatically passes to your spouse and, at that time, a good advisor should recommend your spouse add TOD or POD to the kids.

If your estate is more complicated, and you may not be leaving assets outright to some or all of your children through revocable or irrevocable trust planning, it's imperative that the advisors make sure all assets are titled in the name of that trust. I can't tell you how many times I've met with a new client who has had a trust for some time, and not one single asset is in the name of that trust. In those cases, the trust was done for nothing. The estate will go to probate and may not pass to your children according to your wishes.

Another simple way to avoid probate on a checking or savings account, money market or bank account is to have one or two of your children sign a signature card with the bank, giving them authorization to sign checks in the event of your disability or death. But don't forget to get their signatures on your safety deposit box as well, or no one will be able to access it without those "Letters Testamentary," which means probate.

These are just a couple of simple examples. Estate planning can be very complicated but is less painful with the help of a qualified financial advisor and estate planning attorney.

Again, I remind you, this is a test! This is one of the easiest tests, if you happen to have an account with one spouse's name on it. You may want to purposely change the name of a small account to one spouse to pull this test off effectively. If the advisor totally ignores the fact that you have an account that would cause your spouse to go through probate, leave and never look back.

CHAPTER 13

TEST #4: BENEFICIARY DESIGNATIONS

*What's in a name? That which we call a rose by any
other name would smell as sweet.*

WILLIAM SHAKESPEARE

Those words of Shakespeare's may be fine when it comes
to flowers, but in estate planning, the names in which
assets are titled is of critical importance, with major financial
implications hanging in the balance.

Because of its importance, I purposely separated this type
of "titling" from the previous discussion on estate planning,
even though I feel it is part of proper estate planning. If you
have life insurance policies, IRAs or other retirement plans,
or annuities (fixed or variable), you have the option to list a
primary beneficiary and a contingent beneficiary (the asset
passes to the contingent beneficiary if the primary beneficiary
is deceased). The asset will pass to the beneficiaries upon
your death, outside of probate. As you'll see, it's extremely
important for the advisor to list them correctly.

CASE IN POINT

A woman was referred to me several years ago after
her husband had passed away. She needed help because he
had handled all the finances. As I was going through her
statements and insurance policies, I noticed the primary

beneficiary on the life insurance policy was listed as "Estate." This is one of the biggest no-no's in our industry.

Because a person, namely the wife, wasn't listed as the beneficiary, the insurance policy must go through the probate process, because "estate" means via the will, and all wills must go through probate. The life insurance agent or financial advisor who sold them this policy and failed to list the wife as the beneficiary should, in my opinion, have his or her license revoked. It took more than a year for this woman to get access to that money, and she had three young children to support.

It's equally important for the advisor to suggest that you name a contingent, or several contingent beneficiaries. I've seen many cases in the last twenty-two years where the primary beneficiary dies before the owner of the life insurance policy, annuity, or retirement account does, and their current advisor failed to advise them to update the beneficiary information.

If no contingent beneficiary was named (perhaps because the salesperson was too lazy to fill in all the blanks), then the asset will have to go through probate and pass to the heirs by way of the will or the estate. This creates more legal fees and possibly accelerated income taxes in the case of the retirement accounts.

It's especially important that the advisor properly list beneficiaries on a retirement account. The IRS allows beneficiaries of an IRA to spread or "stretch" an inherited IRA over their own life expectancy (number of years you're expected to live based on mortality tables), which allows them to defer the taxes over a long period of time, if they don't need the money.

Some estate planning attorneys will recommend naming your revocable trust as the beneficiary of an IRA. This may not always be a proper recommendation, because some trusts have wording in them that will disqualify the "stretch IRA" options to the beneficiaries. The easiest explanation is because the IRS does not recognize a trust as having a life expectancy. A good advisor will review your trust, or have an associate attorney review it, to see if there are any concerns about the IRS disqualifying this advantageous option to your children or grandchildren.

> A GOOD ADVISOR WILL REVIEW YOUR TRUST, OR HAVE AN ASSOCIATE ATTORNEY REVIEW IT, TO SEE IF THERE ARE ANY CONCERNS ABOUT THE IRS DISQUALIFYING THIS ADVANTAGEOUS OPTION TO YOUR CHILDREN OR GRANDCHILDREN.

Did you know you can use some of the same estate planning techniques that attorneys use in a will or trust, right on the beneficiary section of a new account application? Unfortunately, many advisors aren't using this technique, perhaps because they're not knowledgeable in estate planning.

Your plan may simply be to pass all of your assets to your spouse upon your death, and then, following your spouse's death, have those assets divided equally among your two children and then to their children. I call this the "I Love You Will" or "Simple Will," which is the most popular way to write a will!

To follow this plan on accounts that name beneficiaries, most advisors will recommend you name your spouse as primary beneficiary and your two children as contingent beneficiaries. This will work fine if the account owner dies first, then the surviving spouse dies, leaving the account to be divided fifty-fifty between the two children.

But what happens if the primary beneficiary, or one of the contingent beneficiaries, dies first? What happens if your two children both have children of their own and you want their share to go to your grandchildren? If the primary beneficiary dies first, a good advisor will recommend the account owner update the primary beneficiary to the two children. However, we still have a problem if one of the two children passes away before the account owner.

CASE IN POINT

A recently widowed mother of two (we'll call her Mary) came to me for advice on her investments, and brought in all her documentation. As I went through the assets which named beneficiaries—IRA account and annuities—I noticed that the two children (we'll call them Paul and Susan) were listed as primary beneficiaries, with each receiving one-half of the accounts at their mother's death.

I asked if she had grandchildren and she said Paul and Susan each had two children of their own, for a total of four grandchildren. She told me that her intention is to have Paul's share of the account go to his children, and Susan's share of the account go to her children, if one of them were to die before her.

I informed her that the way the beneficiaries were currently listed, she may be disinheriting some of her grandchildren. If Paul passed away and then Mary (mom) passed away, the entire account would go to the surviving sibling, which is Susan, thus disinheriting two of her grandchildren (Paul's children).

Even if there was a will that stated Paul's share goes to his children upon Mary's death if he predeceases her, the entire account would still go to Susan, because a beneficiary designation overrides a will. Likewise, if Susan predeceased Mary, the entire account would go to Paul upon Mary's death.

The solution is so easy that I can't believe more advisors don't recommend it. By writing "*per stirpes*" next to the beneficiaries' names in the appropriate section of the account, you'll accomplish the same result as the will would have accomplished, while at the same time avoiding probate (remember, assets that name beneficiaries pass outside of probate).

In the above case, the beneficiary should be listed as Paul, *per stirpes*, 50 percent, and Susan, *per stirpes*, 50 percent. Then Paul's or Susan's share would pass to their own children upon Mary's death, if one of them predeceased her.

This may seem a little complicated to you, but that's why it's so important to make sure you hire an advisor who's knowledgeable in beneficiary designations. Again, this is especially important when naming beneficiaries on IRA accounts, to allow your beneficiaries to utilize the "stretch" options.

This is one of the most important tests! Improperly named beneficiaries can cost your estate and your heirs a lot more time

> THIS MAY SEEM A LITTLE COMPLICATED TO YOU, BUT THAT'S WHY IT'S SO IMPORTANT TO MAKE SURE YOU HIRE AN ADVISOR WHO'S KNOWLEDGEABLE IN BENEFICIARY DESIGNATIONS.

and money in legal fees and taxes, which can easily be avoided by an experienced and knowledgeable financial professional. If the advisors you're interviewing don't bring it up, you may want to ask them how they handle beneficiary designations. If you're not satisfied with their answers, find another advisor.

CHAPTER 14

TEST #5: ACCOUNTABILITY/REVIEWS

An acre of performance is worth a whole world of promise.

ARNOLD J. "RED" AUERBACH

It would be a wonderful thing if our industry could find a way to make all financial advisors and money managers accountable for the recommendations they make. Since there isn't a way to be certain that your advisor is being watched like a hawk by the regulatory agencies, and since most investment recommendations are a matter of opinion anyway, you must have a way to determine if the professional you're working with to handle your life savings is doing a good job. One way is to make them accountable. Don't just accept their initial recommendations and hope for the best. Make them prove it to you time and time again.

The way I make myself accountable to my clients for the recommendations I make is by meeting with them every three months and reviewing their portfolio with them. This review appointment reminds them why they made certain investment decisions. They can see if they're indeed on track to meet the goal each particular investment was meant to accomplish. By comparing their short- and long-term performance against the performance of the market and other similar investments, they can walk away confident they made the right decisions.

The more an advisor meets with you, the easier it is to keep up with changes in your situation. Unexpected events can change things drastically and your financial advisor should be able to guide you in areas where you didn't realize you needed guidance. I advise my clients not to make a financial decision without running it by me first, just in case I think of something they may have overlooked. I've saved many clients money, time, and taxes by recommending other options for their immediate concerns.

CASE IN POINT

Because I meet with my clients often, I'm very aware of their health issues, as well as their financial issues. Recently, one of my clients was diagnosed with cancer and we discussed the issues that needed to be addressed immediately. The cancer took him quickly, but because we made sure everything was titled properly, beneficiary designations were reviewed, accounts were consolidated for the surviving spouse, and legal documents were reviewed and revised according to his wishes, there was very little that had to be done after his death. In fact, his children were very surprised that they didn't have to do a thing.

Many times, I help clients decide whether it's best for them to buy that new car with cash or to finance it. Another popular concern is whether a client should pay off a mortgage or equity line of credit, or keep making payments. The answers to these questions are different for each situation, but my clients know I have an open door policy and can call me whenever they need that type of financial advice.

I don't believe any advisor can keep track of every client's portfolio on a daily or weekly basis. By meeting every three months instead of once a year, which seems to be the norm, the advisor and client can discuss and agree to changes that should be made in the portfolio, if necessary, to adhere more often to market volatility or changes in the client's situation.

The market will go up and the market will go down. Too many times, I've heard from potential clients that they either have to call their representative if they want an appointment to go over their accounts, or their representative suddenly disappears while the market is down.

My office is run like a dentist's office. A client doesn't leave without the next appointment scheduled. Sometimes those appointments will be during bear markets, when people need to be reassured the most.

If you're nearing retirement, or are already retired, you need an investment strategy that takes care of your short-term needs (i.e., new car, vacations, second home, gifting to children, etc.), and your long-term needs (i.e., paying off a home, a

> IF YOU'RE NEARING RETIREMENT, OR ARE ALREADY RETIRED, YOU NEED AN INVESTMENT STRATEGY THAT TAKES CARE OF YOUR SHORT-TERM NEEDS AND YOUR LONG-TERM NEEDS.

trip around the world, grandchildren's college, unexpected medical expenses or nursing home, etc.), while making sure you have the income available now to keep you in the life-style you're accustomed to. Having the ability to increase your income later in case of unexpected expenses or illness, where in-home care or nursing home care may be needed, is crucial for advisors to discuss with you. Basically, you want someone who thinks of everything.

The advisor should discuss how he or she manages risk in your portfolio, and should fill out a risk tolerance questionnaire with you. I believe having the potential advisor fill out this form *with* you enables him or her to delve a little deeper into your past experiences in the market and determine future goals, more than if you're left to fill it out on your own (another mini test).

Some of the questions can be confusing, and you may not answer them correctly, which may distort your true risk tolerance. By doing a little homework, and being aware of some of the different risk management methods, such as stop losses, rebalancing and asset allocation, death benefits, and living benefits (through the use of variable annuities), to mention a few, you can be armed when you interview a new advisor, because you'll have a better understanding of what that person is talking about.

The advisor you choose should meet with you on a regular basis to review your portfolio and keep you up-to-date on its status. Anything less than twice a year is unacceptable. He or she should be very confident in the recommendations they made, while at the same time keeping watch for other opportunities that may help you.

> THE ADVISOR YOU CHOOSE SHOULD MEET WITH YOU ON A REGULAR BASIS TO REVIEW YOUR PORTFOLIO AND KEEP YOU UP-TO-DATE ON ITS STATUS.

Your advisor must be on top of current events, with such unforeseen events as terrorist attacks, dishonest corporate executives, and wars causing havoc in the investment markets. And, with interest rate hikes, inflation/deflation, profit taking and earnings reports, or just talk of these issues affecting the market, it has never been a more important time to make sure your advisor is looking out for your best interests.

If that advisor or a staff member automatically sets up your periodic reviews before you leave the office, then you can't get lost in the shuffle. These meetings will also cause you to become more aware of your financial situation. This includes both spouses, so each of you will feel comfortable with the advisor when one of you passes away or becomes incapacitated.

That advisor passes this test if he or she informs you that there will be multiple reviews of your portfolio during the year, involving both you and your spouse. If the regulatory agencies can't keep advisors accountable, *you* have to do so.

CHAPTER 15

TEST #6: STAFF/ASSOCIATES

No one can whistle a symphony. It takes an orchestra to play it.

HALFORD E. LUCCOCK

A financial advisor who has a staff in direct relation to the number of clients he or she serves should have an office that functions the same way a symphony orchestra does, with its members playing different instruments, but each one complementing and in harmony with all the others.

If I tried to describe the activity that goes on in my office on a daily basis, I could fill another book. I often tell clients that if they spent a week in my office, they'd have a whole new respect for what we have to accomplish.

It also helps if the staff has been together for a while and the turnover is low. Ours is such a highly regulated industry that there's a great deal of paperwork and timely follow-up; it's hard to keep training new people to fill these positions and expect efficiency and few mistakes.

LONE RANGERS

A couple of "professionals" you may want to watch out for are those who work out of the trunk of a car and/or work from home. This is usually a clue that the individual is either new in the business or is a sales representative. The advisor who works from home may be trying to cut expenses, which may be at your expense.

Most of the time, neither of these two types of "planners" has a staff, which means they have to do the marketing, set up appointments, do the advising, complete the paperwork, handle the follow-up and filing, answer phones, conduct research and reviews, monitor accounts, and so on, all by themselves.

How do these individuals do all this in an eight-hour day and remain effective? It's not possible, unless they just sell products, trying to sell as much as possible to as many people as possible.

THE TEAM APPROACH

When you work with retirees, you have to deal with clients passing away, more often than advisors who work with a younger generation. When our office is informed that one of our clients has passed on, one of my assistants will notify me within forty-eight hours that the paperwork has been ordered for death claims, title changes, and beneficiary changes. Another assistant will start working on "date of death" account values for final tax returns.

My secretary will immediately send a card to the spouse or children with condolences from the entire staff, and informing them we're there to help when they're ready. Before meeting with the spouse or other beneficiaries, I'll read through the Will or Trust to start determining distribution of the assets. This system is necessary in order to have these things done in a timely manner.

Clients have often asked me what the scenario would be if something happened to *me*. That's a fair question.

Two of my assistants, who are also licensed representatives, are trained in the products and recommendations I make. Therefore, they're well aware of how and why each client has certain investments.

They're also aware of each client's situation and can handle anything in my absence. We do all our research together, even though I'm the one who makes the recommendations. I'm totally confident in the continuity of the management of our clients' accounts, and the care of those clients should the need arise.

Watch out for the advisors who claim to do everything. By everything, I mean they themselves will do your investments, your taxes, your estate plan, your life insurance, your long term care—you get the picture. Those who do everything themselves simply can't do any of it well. There's not enough time in the day.

> THOSE WHO DO EVERYTHING THEMSELVES SIMPLY CAN'T DO ANY OF IT WELL. THERE'S NOT ENOUGH TIME IN THE DAY.

For example, I feel doing tax returns is a full-time job. A financial advisor who also does tax returns may not be concerned with your investments until after April fifteenth. Likewise, estate tax laws are very complex and require the full attention of an expert estate planning attorney.

Look for an advisor who's affiliated with the other professionals who'll need to be involved in your particular situation. This includes the financial and insurance advisors, attorneys, and accountants. With the team approach, you're more likely to have a plan that works. If not, you may receive conflicting advice that leads to confusion and inaction. This doesn't mean they all have to work out of the same office. I prefer to work with other professionals outside of my practice, just in case one of them doesn't work out one day. Then

> LOOK FOR AN ADVISOR WHO'S AFFILIATED WITH THE OTHER PROFESSIONALS WHO'LL NEED TO BE INVOLVED IN YOUR PARTICULAR SITUATION. THIS INCLUDES THE FINANCIAL AND INSURANCE ADVISORS, ATTORNEY, AND ACCOUNTANTS.

I'm free to recommend someone else. There are firms, however, which have successfully joined forces with other professionals who work well together for the sake of the team.

CASE IN POINT

One of my office staff mentioned that her parents were doing a trust with an attorney I wasn't familiar with, so I suggested she let me read the proposed trust before they signed it. When I did, I was surprised to find someone whose name I didn't recognize as trustee. I was very familiar with her family and asked her who this person was. She didn't know.

Apparently, the attorney who drew up the trust used a "boiler-plated" trust program which allows him to fill in the blanks when he gets a new client. Well, if he misses one of those blanks, it will contain the name of the previous client. Ultimately, her parents ended up having their trust executed by one of the estate planning attorneys I recommended to them.

I like to compare estate planning to health insurance. You never know how good your health coverage is until you need to use it! The same happens with your trust planning. You don't know how good it is until you need to use it—

in which case, you're either incapacitated or dead. I always suggest using someone who specializes in your area of need, which will save you a lot of time and money, along with the aggravation you'll avoid over the long run when mistakes or missed opportunities start to appear.

This test is so crucial. You do *not* want a "salesman" handling your life savings and you do *not* want someone who claims to be all things to all people, with none of it done properly. You also don't want the advisor doing the filing. You want him or her watching your investments, and to have a competent staff. All these tests will help you determine who's a salesman, and who'll be there for the long haul in every aspect of your finances.

Your financial future is much too important to be entrusted to a one-man band. To reach your goals, it takes an orchestra, one that's led by an experienced and well-trained conductor.

Chapter 16

TEST #7: Fees vs. Commissions

Price is what you pay. Value is what you get.

Warren Buffett

There's a big controversy in our industry over whether you're better off working with a financial planner who's a fee-only advisor or a commission-only advisor. You can probably figure out yourself that whenever you see the word "only," you may be missing out on something that may fit your situation nicely but can't be offered by an "only" advisor. "Only" falls in the same category with "never" and "always." Let's see if I can clear up the confusion for you on this topic.

All advisors must have certain licenses to sell certain types of securities in this industry. I choose to carry the licenses which allow me to use any product, regardless of how I'm paid. I don't believe one size fits all, and therefore, I have the ability to match clients up with products that best solve the problems and weaknesses in their financial plan, and help them reach their goals in the best possible way that's available.

If you're going to pay a fee for service, you should make sure it's because you believe you'll be getting extra value from this investment, and from the advisor, which you wouldn't get by buying your own mutual funds, stocks, or bonds. This extra value can mean all the services I've talked about, and/or better performance history. By reviewing your accounts on a regular basis and comparing them to the market indices, you'll be able to judge if the fee you're paying is valuable to you.

> IF YOU'RE GOING TO PAY A FEE FOR SERVICE, YOU SHOULD MAKE SURE IT'S BECAUSE YOU BELIEVE YOU'LL BE GETTING EXTRA VALUE FROM THIS INVESTMENT, AND FROM THE ADVISOR, WHICH YOU WOULDN'T GET BY BUYING YOUR OWN MUTUAL FUNDS, STOCKS, OR BONDS.

I'm no longer surprised by the number of people who don't know if they're paying fees on an account, or what those fees are. Usually, I can find where it was deducted on their quarterly statement and calculate the percentage for them. Some people are surprised at how much their fees have increased over time without their knowledge.

CASE IN POINT

A widowed woman in her eighties was referred to me by one of my clients earlier this year. Her husband, who handled all of the financial affairs, had been deceased for three years. Since she didn't know what else to do, she kept the investments with the advisor her husband had worked with for several years prior to his death.

As I reviewed her statements from the previous three years, I asked her if she was aware that her fees had gradually increased from 1 percent to 2.5 percent over that time. She was unaware of the increase, and unaware that the advisor had taken the nice mutual fund portfolio he had previously set up for them and changed all of it to individual stocks. She had to pay taxes on the sale of the mutual funds, some of which had large gains.

I see this type of situation too many times, when the spouse who handled the investment decisions passes away first. Then everything gets dumped in the lap of the vulnerable surviving spouse, who can easily be taken advantage of. This was one reason for writing this book.

You want to make sure the monthly, quarterly, or annual reports you receive showing your overall performance are shown *net* of the advisor's management fee. That reveals your real rate of increase over a given period of time, *after* all product costs and advisor fees have been deducted.

It is possible to compare two advisors who charge different fees and have the one with the higher fee outperform the one with the lower fee over time. I tell clients who receive comments about the fees they're paying to make sure they compare performance. It's the bottom line that counts.

I recently reviewed a potential client's portfolio, which included a three-year performance report put together by her current advisor. The report showed that her average annual yield for that period was 5.65 percent. She thought this was average and wasn't disappointed until I showed her the fine print, which stated that the returns were reported net of all investment costs, but gross of the advisor's fee. That fee was 1 percent, which has to be deducted, greatly reducing the annual return. Remember, you have to make sure you're getting some extra value by paying someone a fee. This client probably could have done as well, if not better, in an index fund.

There are some products with valuable benefits that may fit your situation but can't be purchased in a fee-based account. These products would fall under the commission category. Certain commission products should not, or cannot, be sold under a fee setup. They can include, but aren't limited to, real estate investment trusts (REIT), limited partnerships (for tax benefits), annuities (fixed and variable), and life insurance.

For example, I come across many situations where a non-publicly traded REIT fits perfectly into a client's portfolio, but should not be under a fee structure, because of the up-front commission paid to the advisor.

One of the most controversial investments in this field is the annuity. Annuities have benefits such as death benefits, living benefits, tax deferral, lifetime income options, diversification (in variable contracts), and beneficiary designations to avoid probate. They can be used in conjunction with a fee account, assuming one part of your portfolio should have the benefits of an annuity, and another part should be fee-based, in order to accomplish two different goals.

However, fee-only and commission-only advisors won't be able to be this creative. You should also be more wary of advisors who just sell annuities. On one hand, they could simply have chosen to specialize in this area, or they could sell them primarily for the commissions involved, and may not have your best interests at heart. By applying all of these tests, you should have a foundation to be able to determine which is which.

I'd like to caution you about using professionals who are strictly life insurance agents and can only sell fixed annuity and life insurance products (unless you're purposely looking for those products). These agents are usually only licensed to sell insurance, and would *not* be a good fit for handling your entire life savings.

I'd also caution you against paying a large up-front fee to an advisor when you have no idea what you're going to get or if you and that advisor will make a good match. I had a prospective client tell me he paid an up-front fee of $20,000 to his last advisor and the relationship didn't last a year.

> I'D ALSO CAUTION YOU AGAINST PAYING A LARGE UP-FRONT FEE TO AN ADVISOR WHEN YOU HAVE NO IDEA WHAT YOU'RE GOING TO GET OR IF YOU AND THAT ADVISOR WILL MAKE A GOOD MATCH.

I believe in the "pay as you go" theory, because if advisors want to keep their fees coming in, they have to keep you informed and happy. This goes along with keeping them accountable. They don't have to be accountable to you if they received a big fee up front with a non-refundable contract.

This test will help you ask the right questions on your interview, to determine if the advisor is limited in what he or she can sell. In summary, you may be better served to work with an advisor who is fee- and commission-based, and who can match you up with the right strategy for your situation, not just sell you a product.

Regardless of whether the advisor works on a fee-only basis, on a commission-only basis, or some combination of the two, it's important that this information is disclosed to you in advance. What's even more important, of course, is to know the character of the individual you're considering. After all, as the great American humorist Will Rogers once reminded us: "It's not what you pay a man, but what he costs you that counts."

CHAPTER 17

TEST #8:
PRODUCT COSTS AND PENALTIES

*Nine-tenths of the serious controversies which
arise in life result from misunderstanding.*

LOUIS D. BRANDEIS

Having served for twenty-three years as a U.S. Supreme
Court Justice, Louis Brandeis was obviously well-
qualified to make the observation quoted above. Austrian
scientist and philosopher Sir Karl Popper was even more
emphatic when he made the following comment: "It is
impossible to speak in such a way that you cannot be
misunderstood." Perhaps it was Popper's comment that gave
rise to the cliché "whatever can be misunderstood will be
misunderstood."

The world of investing is a complex and often confusing
one. Actor Sean Connery was certainly echoing the
sentiments of many folks when he said, "Dealing with this
financial stuff was too much for me." So, whether you're
purchasing a product such as an annuity, mutual fund,
real estate investment trust (REIT), or limited partnership,
to name a few, or if you're retaining a third party
management company, it's important that you eliminate
any misunderstandings about the total costs you're likely to

incur by inquiring if there are any up-front fees, back-end fees, and/or internal or hidden product costs.

As I've already mentioned and will reiterate, I firmly believe that performance, *net* of all fees and expenses, is the *most* important issue, because you can have the same type of portfolio with two different advisors, and one may outperform the other if he or she was more active in managing it.

> COSTS AND PENALTIES SHOULD NOT BE THE BIGGEST DECIDING FACTOR IN CHOOSING A PRODUCT. HOWEVER, YOU SHOULD KNOW WHAT THEY ARE AND AGREE TO THEM.

If your advisor has regular reviews with you and shows you comparisons, you'll see this over time. So costs and penalties should *not* be the biggest deciding factor in choosing a product. However, you should know what they are and agree to them.

Some mutual funds have up-front sales charges, some have contingent deferred sales charges (back-end charges or penalties), and some have both. Make sure you understand why the advisor is using one rather than the other. Some mutual funds have no up-front or back-end charges (also called no-load funds), and are generally used for fee-only accounts. Some funds pay the advisor a trail, which is similar to an ongoing fee, and is built into the expenses of the fund.

CASE IN POINT

I recently analyzed a mutual fund portfolio for a potential client who told me he paid the advisor an annual 1 percent fee, which was deducted from the brokerage account quarterly. I thought the mutual funds that were chosen in this account were pretty good ones. However, I noticed the advisor had purchased "C" shares with this particular mutual fund company. I asked the client if he was aware that the "C" shares were more expensive to own than "A" shares. He said he was not.

I also asked him if he knew the advisor was also getting a 1 percent fee from the mutual funds, which is why this share class is more costly. Of course, he said he was not. Now, this advisor may have had a good reason for investing in this manner, although I can't think of one, but he should have told the client he was "double-dipping."

Most annuities don't have a front-end sales charge, which means 100 percent of your money is invested, but the annuity does carry mortality and expense fees. You may also be paying for certain benefits that have an additional cost added to these fees. If your situation warrants needing those benefits, such as death benefits and/or living benefit, it's perfectly fine to incur those fees, as long as you understand them. Again, regular reviews with your advisor will prove to be valuable, so you can see if you're benefiting from these recommendations.

I'd caution you to also inquire about any contingent deferred sales charges (CDSC), which are charges or penalties to liquidate a mutual fund or annuity over a certain number of years. Sometimes the CDSCs can last for up to ten years or more. The average annuity will have a six-to-eight year CDSC. Anything with a bonus paid to you up front will generally have a longer CDSC.

What this means is that if you need to liquidate the account for any reason, it could cost you a hefty penalty. Products with longer penalty periods may have lower annual expenses, but the commission paid to the salesperson is usually higher. This could be a huge conflict in the recommendation.

Knowing this information ahead of time will give you the opportunity to determine what is more important to you, the lower annual costs, or the flexibility to move to another investment, without a penalty, if something better comes along. It may also help you determine whether this person is a salesman, who just wants to sell a lot of one product and make commissions, or a financial advisor, who's recommending it for the benefits it will add to your portfolio.

There's a very simple test you can use to help determine if the advisor is doing what's in your best interest. Ask if the company whose product he or she is recommending has a shorter CDSC, or if it offers a no-load account (no CDSC). You'd probably shock the advisor, because very few people know you can get the same product from the same company with varying annual expenses and penalty periods. This is most common in the case of purchasing an annuity.

This will force the advisor to explain why he or she recommended the one with the longer penalty. If you don't want to ask the advisor, or if you want to verify the answer you're given, you can call the company's 800 number and find out for yourself. Make sure you received literature on the product so you have the number and exact name of the one being recommended. One phone call can save you a lot of stress later, if you find out you own a product you can't get out of without a huge penalty.

You want to make sure the advisor you're using is conscious of keeping your portfolio as flexible as possible, in case your situation changes, the market changes, or the products being used change. Just as the soap you use today will be "new and improved" tomorrow, the products in our industry will inevitably become cheaper to own, offer better options and/or benefits, or offer better performance opportunities.

I tell my clients I want to keep their accounts flexible so I can change them if something better comes along in my research, without them getting nickel-and-dimed to death.

This is one of the most important tests you can use. If the advisor is making a recommendation—regardless of whether a fee or a commission applies—that you can walk away from without a penalty, you can be pretty confident you're getting the service you deserve, because the advisor will work harder to keep you as a client. Otherwise, you may choose to leave, and the ongoing fees to that advisor will go with you.

> YOU WANT TO MAKE SURE THE ADVISOR YOU'RE USING IS CONSCIOUS OF KEEPING YOUR PORTFOLIO AS FLEXIBLE AS POSSIBLE.

An advisor who receives a commission or fee up front may not be as concerned if you walk out the door, because he or she has already been paid. Always make sure you and the advisor are on the same side of the table. I tell my clients I'm their personal "bird dog." My job is to always be on the lookout for better opportunities and strategies to help them. I'd rather they hear about something better from me than from another advisor!

Chapter 18

Test #9: References

A reputation for keeping absolutely to the letter and spirit of an agreement, even when it is unfavorable, is the most precious of assets.

Lord Chandos

No matter what kind of service you're contracting for, you're always advised to ask for references. Here's my take on that subject: If I give references to prospects, they're probably thinking I've given them my top ten clients, who'll naturally brag about their experience with me. For all you know, they could be family members or close friends. I can guarantee you that no advisor is going to give you the name of an unhappy client. There are other ways to get the information you need to confirm the integrity of the advisor you may want to work with.

I've told potential clients that if I could let them go through my files and pick any client they wanted to talk to, I'd do it. However, because of industry regulations, and my own integrity, the information in those files is highly confidential. So that idea is not an option. Even employees have to be fingerprinted before they can work in a financial planning office, due to the information they have access to.

There are creative ways to get around this problem. Several times a year, I hold client events, such as my annual "Client Appreciation Dinner," where I get my clients together for good food and entertainment. I also hold informational luncheons, and specific product dinners, where I invite a guest speaker from a specific company to keep clients informed and updated about what they own.

> I OFTEN ENCOURAGE POTENTIAL CLIENTS TO ATTEND AS WELL. THIS ALLOWS THEM TO PICK AND CHOOSE THE "REFERENCES" THEY'D LIKE TO TALK TO.

All existing clients are invited to these events, and I often encourage potential clients to attend as well. This allows them to pick and choose the "references" they'd like to talk to. I often joke with potential clients that if my existing clients weren't happy with my services, I'd be crazy to set up events where two hundred of them were together in one room. Their response is usually that it's no joke!

Another way you can get a reference, without the advisor knowing you're doing it, is to call the company which offers the product that was recommended to you and find out who the wholesaler is in that town. People don't realize that wholesalers, the ones who keep advisors informed about performances and changes in the product they represent, visit advisors' offices often and are very aware of who takes care of their clients, who has a high employee turnover, and who invites them to speak to their existing clients in order to keep them informed about what they own.

The test works even better if you ask the wholesaler to recommend several advisors in his or her territory who takes the best care of their clients, but don't name the one you're interviewing. If the name of the advisor you're considering is on the list, you have a great reference. Otherwise, you may want to ask the wholesaler if he or she knows that individual. If not, it may be a clue that the advisor hasn't worked with that product very long, and may be inexperienced with it.

If you're interviewing a good advisor, it's likely that he or she has a busy schedule, meeting with new clients and doing reviews with existing clients. This is actually another test. A busy schedule means the advisor is in demand. Imagine needing a doctor for major heart surgery. Would you want one who has an open schedule and too much free time on his hands?

In any case, when you do get that appointment, you may be sitting in the waiting area with other clients. This is an opportunity to ask them if they're happy with

> IF YOU'RE INTERVIEWING A GOOD ADVISOR, IT'S LIKELY THAT HE OR SHE HAS A BUSY SCHEDULE, MEETING WITH NEW CLIENTS AND DOING REVIEWS WITH EXISTING CLIENTS. THIS IS ACTUALLY ANOTHER TEST. A BUSY SCHEDULE MEANS THE ADVISOR IS IN DEMAND.

the relationship, because it's unlikely the advisor handpicked those who'd be sitting there with you. It's also an opportunity to ask the staff members you encounter how long they've been there. Low turnover can mean the employees are happy with their employer.

This test will help you eliminate the potential conflict of the usual "Top Ten Client Referral List" given by most financial advisors when they're asked for one. However, don't discount the referrals they give you. You may want to talk to a few clients whose circumstances are similar to yours, some who've been clients for a long time, maybe ten years or longer, and a few who've been clients a shorter time, perhaps two to five years. Then make sure you call them! Clients need to be more proactive in picking the person who'll be handling their life savings.

CHAPTER 19

TEST #10:
QUALIFICATIONS/EXPERIENCE

Believe one who has proved it. Believe an expert.

VIRGIL

The technical way to test advisors is to look at their credentials. By that, I don't mean for you to simply check the initials following their names or to be unduly impressed by them. As we explained in chapters one and two, there are dozens of credentials advisors may tack onto their names, but it's extremely important for you to know what they mean and what it took, if anything, for them to earn them.

The advice quoted above from the writings of the Roman poet Virgil are as valid today as they were when he wrote them, more than two thousand years ago. Go beyond the initials and find out if the advisors you're considering truly are experts. Find out what qualifies them to be your advisor. In chapter two, we listed a series of questions which the Securities and Exchange Commission suggests you ask advisors before choosing one. You may want to review them at this point.

For example, it's important to know how long they've been practicing and whether or not they're specialists in the area of planning you require. Naturally, if you're retired or about to retire, you'll want to hire someone who's a retirement specialist.

These specialists should be more knowledgeable about the Social Security system, Medicare, Medicaid, and estate planning. They should also be more up-to-date on the ever-changing tax system and how your retirement accounts will be affected by taxes now and at death (this is a huge issue that would fill another book).

Personally, most of my experience comes from working with retirees and the products available to them for the past twenty-two years. Although the training and continuing education required in our business is a factor, you'll want to hire an advisor who's been working with retirees for some time, preferably longer than ten years. If the choices in your immediate area are limited, you may want to consider traveling a little farther, or even working with someone in another state, if you have a bona fide referral. Thanks to the wonderful technology we have today, distance isn't much of an issue.

> YOU SHOULD CONSIDER HIRING SOMEONE WHO HAS WORKED TO EARN SOME SORT OF DESIGNATION RATHER THAN AN ADVISOR WHO COULDN'T BE BOTHERED TO GO THROUGH THE TRAINING AND TESTING.

An advisor who has chosen to specialize in one area of planning, and has been doing so for many years, should have already encountered most situations, including those which you may be in. He or she should be pretty confident with the recommendations that have worked best for clients in similar situations.

As you read the information in the section of chapter one titled "Alphabet Soup," it's very confusing to determine what all those letters after an advisor's name mean, and how significant they are. You should consider hiring someone who has worked to earn some sort of designation rather than an advisor who couldn't be bothered to go through the training and testing, and doesn't want to keep up with the continuing education required with most designations.

To my knowledge, the Certified Financial Planner (CFP) designation requires the most education to earn the license to

> It's HARD ENOUGH TO FIND ONE PLANNER WITH ALL OF THESE QUALIFICATIONS, BUT WHEN YOU DO, YOU WON'T NEED ANOTHER ONE.

use those prestigious letters. It takes an average of two years to acquire them, and is one of the most stringent when it comes to continuing education. It would be a good start if you found an advisor who's a CFP, as the CFP Board of Standards is very strict about allowing advisors to retain this designation in the event of disciplinary actions.

If you discover that an advisor you're considering has experienced a less than desirable disciplinary action, this alone doesn't signify dishonesty or incompetence. Sometimes the system, just like the law, isn't always fair. You can ask the advisor to explain any discrepancies and decide whether or not to accept their explanation. In such cases, find out if that advisor still has their CFP designation. The CFP Board *must* be apprised of all complaints from the public, and if the advisor was found guilty of doing something corrupt or dishonest, the CFP designation would have been withdrawn.

Case in Point

At an interview with potential clients, I listened to their experience of losing all of the money they put in three different investments with the same advisor. I asked them if they had received a prospectus for any of the three investments,

> The Certified Financial Planner (CFP) designation requires the most education to earn the license to use those prestigious letters. It takes an average of two years to acquire them, and is one of the most stringent when it comes to continuing education.

which they had not. After researching the advisor's credentials, I found he'd been stripped of his securities license and his CFP designation for selling unregistered securities.

He's still holding public seminars, but not disclosing that he now only carries a life insurance license. I'm sure you guessed that he'd be recommending only insurance products if you worked with him now. This book should help you avoid such unethical advisors.

It's easier to accomplish this test after you meet with a potential advisor. It would be impossible to list all the designations, and explanations of what they mean, in this book. However, after you meet with a potential candidate, you can go online and look up the designation to find out what kind of training was, and continues to be, required to keep those credentials.

CHAPTER 20

THE ROAD AHEAD

*Nobody can really guarantee the future. The best
we can do is size up the chances, calculate the
risks involved, estimate our ability to deal with them
and then make our plans with confidence.*

HENRY FORD II

My purpose in writing this book isn't to frighten you,
but to help you steer clear of the pitfalls and potholes
that might otherwise foil your plans as you make the journey
toward a comfortable future. After reading it for the first
time, you may be feeling a bit overwhelmed with all this
information. Therefore, please read at least the Top Ten
Tests several times before you start interviewing prospective
advisors. Before meeting with them, you can get some of
this information, such as their designations, from their
advertisements or seminars.

In fact, it's not too late to test your *current* financial
advisor. These ten tests can be accomplished without alerting
the advisor to what you're doing. You just have to open your
eyes and know what to look for. I've heard over and over
again, "But he's such a nice person," or, "I've been with her
so long," and, "That's who my spouse (or parents) used."

Nearly all financial professionals are nice people; but are
they doing the whole job, or will they end up costing you

more in taxes? Will they hurt your estate more than help it in the event of a major market correction, illness, or death of one or both spouses? The problem is, by the time you find out, it's too late. Using these tests can at least increase your chances of a better outcome.

It's a bonus to find a planner who's very creative in making recommendations. With all the products and strategies available to the professionals who take the time to learn them, you may get better results across the board in your overall financial plan, which includes tax planning, estate planning, retirement planning, insurance planning, and investment planning. All these things have to work together, and you can't change one without affecting the others.

That's why it's so difficult to work with more than one advisor in different companies. The first one may have you going in one direction and the second in another, which could create chaos in your overall plan. It's hard enough to find one planner with all of these qualifications, but when you do, you won't need another one.

If you conduct the Ten Tests and find an advisor who passes most of them, I can assure you you've come closer to working with someone who'll be more creative and knowledgeable about all areas of financial planning than an advisor who thinks only one way, and has every client invested the same way. Under no circumstances should you get advice from one advisor and implement it with another one, because the advisor doing the investing doesn't have to be accountable for someone else's recommendations.

Going it Alone

To those who do their own investing, I strongly recommend that you start building a solid relationship with a competent advisor anyway. If you believe in Murphy's Law, then the possibility exists that the spouse who handles the money will become too ill to continue, or will be the first to pass away, with everything dumped into the lap of the survivor.

That's *not* a good time to start looking for someone to take care of the surviving spouse. I've personally seen how badly widows and widowers get taken advantage of when they're in that situation. If you have the relationship built already, the advisor will be familiar with the situation and can help your spouse with the least amount of stress. In fact, your estate should already have been set up to continue to support your spouse with minimal changes.

> THE POSSIBILITY EXISTS THAT THE SPOUSE WHO HANDLES THE MONEY WILL BECOME TOO ILL TO CONTINUE, OR WILL BE THE FIRST TO PASS AWAY, WITH EVERYTHING DUMPED INTO THE LAP OF THE SURVIVOR.

In the Dark

One of my goals with this book is to start improving society's ignorance about money and finances. I'm sad to say that, of all the people I've met in the last twenty-two years, 80 percent of them couldn't tell me what they were worth before I did their "Financial Physical." Many clients I see have assets all over the place, with no real strategy. The more complicated their plan is, the harder it is to determine if it is working and what it's earning.

Most clients can't tell me what the past performance has been of any of their investments, or their overall portfolio. In fact, a lot of people can't even tell me if they're paying fees on their accounts or, if they do, what those fees are!

I strongly disagree with all the "financial experts" you see on TV who advise you to "do it yourself, and stay away from all those commission hungry advisors who want to take advantage of you." You can only get taken advantage of if you stay ignorant about your finances, and don't do your homework before hiring a professional. Besides, you should never sign anything unless you totally understand how it works and what it's supposed to do for you.

> YOU CAN ONLY GET TAKEN ADVANTAGE OF IF YOU STAY IGNORANT ABOUT YOUR FINANCES, AND DON'T DO YOUR HOMEWORK BEFORE HIRING A PROFESSIONAL.

If you're just looking to pick one mutual fund to throw some money into, then maybe you can do it yourself. But, if you're trying to accomplish everything I've brought up in this book, you'll have to get your hands on a tremendous amount of information and conduct your own research and comparisons. Then you have to constantly monitor your progress. This can become another full-time job at a time in life when you should be enjoying the fruits of your labor.

In reality, of the seventy-eight million or more baby boomers, how many *will* actually do it themselves? There'll be over twenty million of them retiring over the next five years and seeking the help of a professional they can trust to help keep them financially independent, and then help their families after they're gone.

So, it's safe to say I'm on a mission to change the quality of financial advice given to prospective clients, especially those who've reached that stage in life where they're no longer accumulating money, but using it. This means the baby boomers who are nearing retirement, are already retired, and who are most at risk of outliving their income and having to deal with expensive health issues.

GET MORE INVOLVED

You *must* become more involved in your own finances and know what your expenses are. You *must* do your homework when hiring someone to help you with the intricacies of investing. Your due diligence will help to improve the quality of these professionals if they want to get and keep your business.

Integrity, honesty, experience, credentials, competency, and creativity are obviously the traits we want in the professionals who handle the financial part of our lives. Although money doesn't buy happiness, we can't live without it. The person you hire should be involved in your life for a long time.

If enough people in this country read this book and pass it on to others they care about, a lot of incompetent advisors and the salesmen in our industry will be forced to step up to the plate and take the time to educate themselves and acquire the knowledge and experience necessary to pass my Ten-Test policy. I hope new advisors entering our business will heed my advice, because we need more competent advisors to help the millions of baby boomers who'll be searching us out over the next decade.

How comforting it would be to go to sleep at night knowing your affairs are in order, with your assets being cared for properly:

✓ giving you the most flexibility when things change

✓ consolidating more as you get older so you can understand what you own, why you own it, and how it's performing

✓ knowing you're taking advantage of all the IRS offers you to save on taxes now, and at your death, when the assets pass to your heirs

✓ the ability to live on the income you need now and have room to increase that income in case of unexpected expenses or future illnesses

✓ that all your accounts are titled properly and beneficiaries are listed correctly to simplify the distribution of these assets upon your death and help eliminate the need for an attorney and probate

✓ knowing your wills, trusts, health care proxies, and powers of attorney are all up-to-date

✓ that you have enough and the right kind of insurances to take care of you if you're ill, and take care of your family upon your death

✓ and, most importantly, that your spouse (and/or your children) will be "okay" financially when you're gone

Do you really want to do all of this yourself?

I know I've brought up a lot of issues you probably never thought of. Basically, there's a lot more to financial planning than just picking investments. That's why you need a good, competent, caring investment professional who's qualified and objective. Doing your homework can be very time-consuming, but you have a great deal at stake, so it's well worth the effort.

Once you've identified a planner who qualifies in each of these ten areas, have satisfied yourself as to that planner's character and competency, and feel comfortable with him or her, you're well on your way to the long-range financial security that's so important to you and your family.

> INTEGRITY, HONESTY, EXPERIENCE, CREDENTIALS, COMPETENCY, AND CREATIVITY ARE OBVIOUSLY THE TRAITS WE WANT IN THE PROFESSIONALS WHO HANDLE THE FINANCIAL PART OF OUR LIVES.